I0160549

The Bible is honest about suffering. For Crying Out Loud is a book of forty meditations that focus on loss and recovery. Everyone is affected by loss so that we are all opened up to suffering. Relational suffering, in particular, goes very deep. King David understood relational suffering. Some of his psalms are bold in saying how much we hurt, and are hurt by, other people.

This book of meditations provides an opportunity to hear biblical cries of the heart. Underlying the words on every page is a hope that you will be able to connect so deeply with what is said in scripture that you sense more clearly what goes on in your own heart and also realize that painful experiences are felt and named by other people, some who lived thousands of years ago.

Scripture shows us that, for various reasons that are human and divine, we need to cry out to the Lord when we are in pain, confused, lost or frightened. We cry when we no longer can bear loss in silence. It may be that pain has pushed us far into silence—inexpressible and unbearable. Yet even paralyzing sorrow may move as we cry out loud—numbness can waken into lament. A cry for help is heard by a God who never tires of hearing the voice of one who seeks God's face.

Spend time in these pages. As you read, you will see patterns in loss, suffering and recovery that allow you to comfort those caught up in a crisis or explain something which is happening to you. Joyce Bellous' aim in writing the book is to encourage you to understand loss and suffering so that you enjoy life in Christ Jesus more abundantly and are able to live more wisely in the world.

Joyce E. Bellous is Associate Professor of Lay Empowerment and Discipleship at McMaster Divinity College in Hamilton Ontario, where she has taught since 1993. She is an educational consultant and teaches in the areas of religious education and ministry education. Since 1997, she has directed the Parish Nurse Institute, which has over 200 graduates. Joyce addresses issues of spirituality, ethics, postmodernism, multiculturalism and leadership. Her recent book, *Educating Faith*, approaches spiritual formation from a Christian perspective. She is currently involved in research into Christian character education.

FOR CRYING OUT LOUD

FOR CRYING OUT LOUD

40 Meditations on Loss and Recovery

JOYCE E. BELLOUS

TALL PINE PRESS

© 2008
TALL PINE PRESS
94 - 11215 Jasper Ave
Edmonton AB T5K 0L5
Canada

FOR CRYING OUT LOUD
Written by Joyce E. Bellous

All rights reserved. No part of this book may
be reproduced or copied in any form without
written consent from the publisher.

Scripture quotations taken from the HOLY BIBLE
NEW INTERNATIONAL VERSION.
Copyright © 1973, 1978, 1984 by International Bible Society.
First published in Great Britain 1979
Inclusive language version 1995, 1996
Used by permission of Hodder & Stoughton,
a member of the Hodder Headline Group.
All rights reserved.

Printed in the United States.

Design: Dianne Eastman
Front Cover Photography: Noel Powell
Back Cover Photography: Rhienna Cutler

Library and Archives Canada Cataloguing in Publication
Bellous, Joyce Edith, 1948-
    For crying out loud : 40 meditations on loss and recovery / Joyce E. Bellous.
ISBN 978-0-9810149-0-6
1. Loss (Psychology)–Religious aspects–Christianity–Meditations.
2. Suffering–Religious aspects–Christianity–Meditations.
3. Healing–Religious aspects–Christianity–Meditations.
4. Suffering–Biblical teaching. 5. Christian life–Meditations. I. Title.

BV4905.3.B45 2008   242'.4   C2008-903371-X

DEDICATION

Many conversations went into writing these meditations. My desire was to help us understand human suffering more adequately. The book is dedicated to those who are committed to being healers—and to all those who long to be well. Dan Johnson read the manuscript, making precise and helpful comments. I am sorry he is not here to see the book. Many people helped as I wrote and thought about loss and recovery. In particular, thanks to Carol-Anne Mackness, Meghan McIntosh, Iris Bogle, Cindy Westfall, who read the manuscript and opened up new insights for me and to Ann Trousdale for conversation and insight. I especially want to thank Dianne Eastman for all that transpires through enduring friendship.

CONTENTS

PREFACE

In April 2005 I stood by the Wailing Wall in the city of Jerusalem—a site I wanted to visit for a long time. I saw stones that have lain together for over 2000 years. They were there when Jesus entered the city. I looked to my left and my right and sensed the passion people who approached the wall brought with them. A full range of emotions, hopes, dreams, requests, complaints and lament were written on bits of paper, pressed into crannies and cracks in a wall of rocks.

As I stood by the Wall, I recalled cries of the heart recorded in scripture and remembered a thesis written by one of my students that I just finished reading before this trip. Her topic was spiritual liberation and she analyzed the important role of crying out loud to the Lord as part of a process of healing. For various reasons, human and divine, we need to cry out to the Lord when in pain, confused, lost or frightened. We cry when we can no longer bear loss in silence. There is also pain that pushes us further into silence—inexpressible suffering, more than bearable.[1] Yet even paralyzing losses are unfettered as we cry out loud—numbness can awaken into lament.

Perhaps this book of meditations is like a Wailing Wall. It is an invitation to cry out to God. It can be a holy place for women and men to seek and find sanctuary, a place to express desires of the heart. It is an encounter that is public, private, shared and secret. Underlying these devotions on loss and recovery is my hope that you will be able to connect so deeply with sentiments in scripture that you are able to identify what is going on in your heart and realize your experience is named and felt by other people, some who lived thousands of years ago. As you read, perhaps a period of paralysis that has become a normal part of life will break in tears, anger, feelings that spark life in all those who finally call out to a God who is never offended by cries of the heart.

This book invites you to stand on Holy Ground, which is a place within us we eventually find if finally and fully we lament our losses. The book offers divine and human reasons to cry out to a God who hears us and keeps our tears in a bottle because they are precious (Psalm 56:8). God is a willing listener and does not tire of hearing from us. (Luke 18:1-8) It is confidence in God that I hope these meditations will inspire. As you read these meditations I hope you are sustained by the marvellous grace of God who sees and hears your cries for help.

The meditations in this book are based mostly on what I call psalms of opposition, thirty psalms drawn together because of their focus on loss and recovery. I want to be clear about the suffering these pages describe. We are accustomed in Western culture to think of suffering primarily as a psychological experience—something that happens to a particular person for specific reasons. If we focus on suffering as psychological only, like Job's friends, we come to blame the sufferers, believing that their sorrow is a justifiable result of personal sin and conclude they are getting what they deserve. While we may not express this belief overtly, we turn away from those who suffer and wait for them to get over it so that everyone can get back to normal life.

But suffering is more than merely psychological. Psalms of opposition present a complex picture of suffering, though they are full of psychological insight and depth. For one thing, they speak to the truth that normal life is full of suffering. Sorrow has many faces and multiple causes that are not easily untangled. Harm is woven into the human condition. Its warp works down through generations; its woof fills in patterns in ordinary life that make no sense at a personal level alone. David the psalmist understood this human reality. In Jewish and Christian traditions, David is the acknowledged author of the thirty poems I single out as psalms of opposition.[2] I refer to him throughout these meditations, assuming they convey aspects of his life that rely on the texture, shape and colour of the story we know of him.

David knew that suffering was a sociological reality, in addition to being deeply personal. With him, we realize that we suffer from jolts so deep-going we cannot resume ordinary life until we make some sense of what happened. We are shocked when social rules we counted on, took for granted as secure, are violated. Jolts come in many forms—violation in the privacy of a child's bedroom, shunning in a workplace environment due to the hardness of people's hearts. Suffering is an aftermath of social trauma—of jolts that disturb us in ways we are unable to address when they happen. The psalms of opposition recount personal and sociological wars that rage in every society. David named his suffering and brought his angst to God.

Some of the meditations you will read also rely on insights from the book of Ezekiel due to its theme of loss and recovery. Other insights come from the book of Job. Some insight comes from educational theory and social science research whenever these disciplines illuminate the human patterns involved in experiencing loss and recovering from it. Woven through all the meditations is an unwavering confidence that suffering is perceived by God and makes sense in his kingdom. That confidence finds its expression in the belief that none of us can fall out of his grasp.

Every human being must address loss. Earth is not heaven. Loss is natural—all learning is driven by loss and recovery. But sometimes, losses are too enormous for the human personality to bear. Those who suffer are traumatized rather than educated by them, at least initially. It is trauma I pray the book will address. I hope nothing I write minimizes suffering but rather, shows how it operates. I point to the marks suffering leaves in the soul and on the body. Those who know the New Testament will hear echoes of Jesus' words in the psalms of opposition. Those who long to know him better will find renewed insight into his suffering and victory over death. All the meditations in this book explore unexpected experiences in a Christian life. The book is a call to move deeply into Jesus' life, death, resurrection and his continuous presence as the primary way to make sense of the world.

Rebellion or Recovery

> The Lord looks down from heaven on the
> human race to see if there are any who
> understand, any who seek God.
>
> **Psalm 14:2**

To meditate on scripture is to receive an invitation—one you may not want to accept. In order to reflect on the topic of loss and recovery, as your devotion to God, you need to be willing to ask yourself a question. Just as Jesus asked the man by the pool of Bethesda, he asks you now: Do you want to be whole? (John 5:1-15) I hope you are quick enough to ask other questions that the man by the pool did not think to ask: "Jesus, what is being whole like? What would it mean for me to be well?" Jesus made the man well so he could experience being whole. What is it like to be well? The answers to that question are found throughout scripture. To be well is to know God. Jesus said, "Now this is eternal life: that they may know you, the only true God, and Jesus Christ, whom you have sent." (John 17:3) God wants communion with humankind as a start for healing.

God's desire for our wholeness runs throughout scripture. The Old Testament book of Ezekiel is a marvellous exploration of rebellion and recovery, threads you can trace through its pages. God wants people to know him. This desire is expressed repeatedly. Everything

God asked Ezekiel to do or say was aimed at conveying this point. The signs, messages, even the punishment aimed at one purpose: that the people might know God. But we read that they were rebellious. What was their rebellion like? What did they do wrong? If eternal life is to know God, what is sin? Ezekiel revealed God's description of human rebellion. "The word of the Lord came to me: Son of man, you are living among a rebellious people. They have eyes to see but they do not see and ears to hear but they do not hear, for they are a rebellious people." (Ezekiel 12:1-2) Why are seeing and hearing so important? What does it mean to see and to hear? Seeing and hearing are so basic to ordinary living. Doesn't God want us to do something much harder than use our eyes and ears to perceive him? Anyone can see and hear.

What does God want from you? He wants faith, best described as knowing him—seeing and hearing the world, yourself—the way God sees and hears. Faith leads us to open our eyes and unplug our ears so we can experience God and observe what God is doing. The main reason you might not want to accept the invitation to meditate on loss and recovery, the main obstacle to realizing that faith is a way of seeing and hearing, is that following God opens us up to suffering as well as to blessing. Jesus was honest when, in the Beatitudes, he said suffering and joy work together in a life of faith. (Matthew 5:1-12)

People of faith are willing to let God show them the world. Earth is not heaven. Therefore, the seeing and hearing of faith is touched by pain at times and with responsibility always. But when we perceive that it is so, everything that happens, whether suffering at the hands of other people, or the pain of being stalled in our own thoughts, is blessed by knowing that nothing can separate us from the love of God. Our losses and recoveries are the means by which we come to know God more fully, even as we are fully known by God. This is as good as it gets—God be praised.

Lord Jesus, let me see that you love me.

Let me feel you are near. I understand in my head

that knowing you is what I want.

Let me feel it in my heart. Allow me to perceive

my own blindness, my deafness.

This is a strange thing to ask perhaps.

I am somewhat frightened by it.

I am not sure where you will take me,

but I am tired of where I am.

Lord, please come to help me. Amen

Kingdom People

In reply Jesus declared, "I tell you the truth,
no-one can see the kingdom of God without
being born again....Flesh gives birth to
flesh, but the Spirit gives birth to spirit."

John 3:3, 6

Born again? Jesus was speaking to Nicodemus when he spoke this message. Nicodemus came to see Jesus at night. He was a religious leader of the Jewish ruling council, important and learned. He saw in Jesus something attractive, a quality or power he did not have, though he was rich in worldly and religious terms. Jesus' miraculous signs uncovered the man's poverty of sight. He was confused and interested. He came to a Rabbi that puzzled him. He knew Jesus came from God (John 3:2) but he was so different! They had a remarkable conversation. In talking together, Jesus unveiled his mission to be lifted up so "everyone who believes in him may have eternal life." (John 3:15) These verses do not say what affect the conversation had on Nicodemus, but later we learn he supported Jesus during a Council meeting (John 7:50) and came to get Jesus' body after the Crucifixion. (John 19:39) That first encounter invited Nicodemus to consider the possibility of following Jesus despite the personal threat involved in seeking him out.

During their conversation, our Saviour said, "For God so loved the world that he gave his one and only Son...whoever believes in him shall not perish but have eternal life." (John 3:16) Christians memorize this verse in childhood. But experiences in church, at work or at home may force us to question whether accepting Jesus' offer of salvation pays out in lives that convey that "Spirit gives birth to spirit." Scripture says "the fruit of the Spirit is love, joy, peace, patience, kindness, goodness, faithfulness, gentleness and self-control." (Galatians 5:22) If Spirit gives birth to spirit, wouldn't we see in Christian leaders, teachers, parents and friends evidence of the Holy Spirit's presence in their inner being? Is that what we see? Sometimes we do. Yet people who claim to be Christian also fail to live out the power of Christ so that those they love suffer. If believers fail to be like Jesus, their failure leaves devastating wounds in the people that are dependent on them—wounds not easily healed, memories that trouble dreams and daily life.

Loss is inevitable in a life of faith. When we suffer loss, its effects do not signal that we are alone or strange. Our suffering is common to humanity. We take comfort from scripture because it tells the truth about human experience and does not cover up sins that even strong believers commit. Scripture urges us to focus on "whatever is true, whatever is noble, whatever is right, whatever is pure, whatever is lovely, whatever is admirable—if anything is excellent or praiseworthy—think about such things." (Philippians 4:8) Scripture tells the truth and also invites us toward maturity.

We want to follow its guidance. Yet in focusing on what is worthy, we are also compelled to face what is sinful. What can we expect from sinners saved by grace? What can we hope for our own faithful lives? We must read scripture carefully. Do we enjoy the fruit of the Spirit in company with other believers? We must *learn* to live scripture faithfully.

Lord, I am terrified to look at loss and recovery. I don't want to think

about my disappointments. I would rather be angry, depressed—at least that I can understand. How can I face the possibility of really living in the Spirit? What if I continue to be sad or angry? What if nothing changes? Yet I will trust that you have met people like me before. I am not alone, not strange. You know what to do with me, though I do not know what to do with myself. Help my unbelief. Speak with me like you did with Nicodemus. I am confused and afraid. Don't leave me in the condition I am in today. Have mercy, Lord. Let me sense your presence. I am here to talk with you about the losses in my life.

No One Came For Me!

Though my mother and father forsake me,
the Lord will receive me.

Psalm 27:10

There are many ways for parents to abandon children. In Israel, I got an impression that children are important to parents and to the whole culture. When the psalmist said God would receive him even if his parents forsook him, I think he built a worst case scenario, almost unimaginable in a culture in which parents were dependent on children in their old age. As I observed interactions on streets, or in kibbutzim, I couldn't believe those parents would forsake their children. We also went to the Holocaust Museum and visited the children's exhibit. It was a suspended walkway. Around me there was no light except for tiny bright, electric stars. As I moved through darkness, a voice spoke, relentlessly naming each child lost to the future of Israel. I was struck by a sense of utter desolation due to losing those little ones in concentration camp horrors.

A friend told me this story. She recalls being in a campground as a tiny child, three years old. It had a beach with access through the woods. One afternoon she and her two older brothers went to the beach, following their father. Close to the woods, her father started to run. She tried to keep up in her little flip flop sandals. Somehow her brothers managed. Her father led through a patch of mud just before entering the woods. Her brothers negotiated it and kept running. As she ran into it she got stuck, sinking ankle-deep in mud sucking at her feet. She screamed for help. No one came. Close by, a family spotted her terror. She remembers the boy's name, Billy. He attended her brother's karate class. His mother pulled her out of the mud. She remembers a large towel the woman wrapped her in before she washed her feet with warm water. She can't say how long it was before her family realized her absence. Billy's mom got water hot in a campground, brought a towel, washed mud off little feet—that took a long while. She knows Billy's mom was kind but no one is mother or father at three years old except our own parents. They did not come. She told the story like any survivor: by her facial expression, I saw she was in back in the camp, stuck in mud. It is one of many stories she can tell.[3] Abandoned children feel these losses. When adults forsake them, their losses create unresolved tension for children—pressure that troubles all their relationships until they are restored through new experiences with Christ and other people.

The young need more than an attentive adult to run with them to the beach. They need parents to remain faithful to them throughout life. Contrary to the pop culture savvy of the 1960s in North America, that free-loving, free-wheeling era of individualism, children of divorce suffer different and more difficult grief than children whose parent dies.[4] When adults remain in place, it is as if the young can grow up healthily, by checking back with people who remain a constant point of contact.[5] If adults remain, children are able to reconcile and recover a sense of balance essential for maturity. In normal experience, what we separate from we can find anew.[6] But if our home environment is lost during childhood, loss can be so great it is impossible to recover balance; depression may result. It is a common insight "that the underlying substrate of depression is loss."[7] To lose home is to lose part of oneself: if home disappears during childhood, physically or emotionally, it may leave us with unrecoverable loss, confirming our worst suspicions about life. Stuck in mud, we cannot move forward, unless someone comes.

Lord Jesus, I am stuck in mud sucking at my feet, unable to get free.

Pull me out. Wash my feet, as you did with the disciples. Let me know

that you run with me to the beach and will wait. I imagine the beach

where you made breakfast for your disciples. I want to run with you to

that place of refreshment but my feet don't seem to be moving.

Lord, please release me from the place where my feet are stuck.

Household Losses—Household Gains

A wife of noble character who can find?
She is worth far more than rubies. Her
husband has full confidence in her and
lacks nothing of value. She brings him
good, not harm, all the days of her life.

Proverbs 31:10-12

How can we understand loss? It is an understatement to say households have changed since the 1950s. Something was lost. What is it? What is a household? How are we to relate to others so that the needs of a small group of biologically linked individuals flourish as a household of faith? Men have changed; women have changed; children have changed. What are we to do with outcomes of an upheaval that is hard to measure? I wonder if one of the main losses we experience in our homes is the courage to tell the truth. Yet, perhaps, there never was a time when it was easy to tell the truth to people in whose company we are utterly vulnerable. Because gender rules have changed, there is more confusion about the difficulty of telling the truth in our families. We often lie to those we love. Hannah Arendt named one of our lies. She was a Jewish philosopher in the early twentieth century. She loved Heidegger, a German philosopher, one of her teachers. She sent him a book she wrote, titled, *The Human Condition*. He never responded. She wrote to Carl Jaspers, another teacher, to comment on Heidegger's silence and unveiled a common pattern in women that

I know. She said,

> I knew that [Heidegger] finds it intolerable that my name
> appears in public, that I write books etc. All my life I've
> pulled the wool over his eyes, so to speak, always acted
> as if none of that existed and as if I couldn't count to
> three, unless it was in the interpretation of his own
> works. Then he was always very pleased when it turned
> out that I could count to three and sometimes even to
> four. Then I suddenly felt this deception was becoming
> just too boring, and so I got a rap on the nose. I was very
> angry for a moment, but I am not any longer. I feel instead
> that I somehow deserved what I got—that is, both for hav-
> ing deceived him and for suddenly having put an end to it.[8]

Arendt identifies a trap we get tangled in when we marry. We are
partly something we do not reveal. Is it an act of love to reveal only
what others can easily bear about us and hide the rest? How does
opposition work in families? I suggest that it plays out forcefully since
our need for and threat from family members goes very deep. People
we love may oppose our happiness. Personal happiness is a desire
that things should go mostly the way we want. Conflict erupts if opposition is not adequately addressed. But if people grow up without *any*
opposition, they become insular and fail to ask about others' wishes
when making plans. Tyrants eradicate opposition to getting their own
way. Arendt minimized conflict in her relationship by shutting down
opposition not through force, but by not telling the truth. Her talent
was a truth she assumed Heidegger could not bear. Women in particular, often don't act as smart as they are. Tension between hiding and
telling the truth is important to understand if we hope to become people of faith, if we want to learn to live together well and love one
another as Jesus loves us.

In psalms of opposition, David began by telling God the truth about himself. We don't know whether he told the truth to others, but scripture calls us to speak the truth. Truth is a good we bring to others, even if it intensifies opposition at the start.

Jesus, help me sense hypocrisy when I fear the people I say I love.

Let me see how loving them includes telling the truth. I need your

wisdom—I haven't been honest. I don't know where to begin.

Lord, please help me come out of hiding.

What do Men Want?

David continued up the Mount of Olives,
weeping as he went; his head was covered
and he was barefoot.

2 Samuel 15:30

David was shaken. He went up to the room over the gateway and wept. As he went, he said: O my son Absalom! My son, my son Absalom! If only I had died instead of you—O Absalom, my son, my son! (2 Samuel 18:33)

In graduate school, I heard the story of a young woman, a lesbian journalist, who wanted to find out what happens at Promise Keepers' meetings. She dressed as a young man, with a sock in the appropriate place, as she put it, to attend a meeting. She related her discomfort with some of what was said from the podium, but she also said that, as they stood to sing, two older men on either side of her grasped her hands. She reported that, standing between them as they sang and wept—she had never felt so loved. Are these gatherings of men a corporate lament like King David's? Are they an opportunity to cry out loud over what gets lost during the wars of daily life as men strive for victory over money, power, sex, position—competitions of every kind—games that lead to using people they proclaim to love as pawns in the moves they make?

What did men lose in twentieth century? What do they regain by gathering together to sing and weep? King David lost Absalom. His loss had its roots in his own sin: he seduced Bathsheba—Uriah's wife—a woman he had no need for. His household was full of women. He covered up his transgression by having Uriah killed in a foolish battle maneuver. (2 Samuel 11) Later, he failed to respond morally and righteously to the rape of Tamar, when Amnon took her against her will and after violating her, cast her aside. Absalom was her brother (2 Samuel 13:1) and he killed Amnon in revenge. David neglected that family feud until Absalom began a rebellion against his father that led to the son's death. Circulating loss, unending harm, relentless sorrow stemming from failure to act ethically is a story for many men's lives. The trap of being male has to do with being caught reaching for what is not essential to life, using means that enslave those who grasp at small, vain, passing fascinations—delicacies that leave a bad taste in the heart.

I recall a young man who came to me after I spoke at a conference to confess his addiction to pornography. We wept together and prayed. He also wondered aloud why his Christian group had so many women and so few men. I didn't say it, but I imagined them sitting in front of their own computers, like him, engrossed in experiences that steal time and energy, with nothing left for God, though, like him, they profess faith. What does it mean to be manly? How are losses to be recovered when everything we hear and see drives in one direction: acquiring position, sex, money, power, privilege? What would happen if we let go of what goes along with our place in society? What counts as loss? Are we losers if we give away what we do not need? Can we stop measuring ourselves against the accomplishments of others and still have something to respect in ourselves?

Lord, I have no idea what would happen if I let go of striving for more,

if I stopped rushing after reputation, social respect, if I no longer had the answers to everyone's problems? I don't know what others would think if I didn't laugh at their crude jokes. Why do I laugh when others get hurt, as if getting hurt doesn't matter or should be laughed off? How can I stop racing through every day? What would happen if I told a friend I wasn't busy and had time for his friendship? I haven't taken time to count my losses. I try not to think about them. I want them to go away. Yet I keep making the same mistakes over and over. I'm out of control. I want you, Lord, to control me—but I know you require my cooperation. Help me see how to give it.

Awaiting Return

Tax collectors and 'sinners' were all
gathering round to hear him....Pharisees
and the teachers of the law muttered,
'This man welcomes sinners, and eats
with them.'

Luke 15:1-2

I was listening to a sermon on the Lost Son. It was a winsome word urging us to focus on finding the lost. I agreed with the preacher. Yet my mind took a turn when hearing these stories of lost sheep, lost coins and lost children. I have always understood Jesus to be pointing out the need to find the lost. After all, Pharisees and teachers of the law were criticizing him for eating with the sinners, something a rabbi should not do. Rabbis were supposed to know better than to eat with the unworthy. Teachers were to discern the clean from the unclean and keep their outward life pure. But Jesus wanted to focus on the inner life—to keep it pure as well.

Focusing on clean or unclean items and actions and Jesus' desire for people to look inward was not what caught my attention when listening to that sermon. Instead, I saw a difference between sheep, coins and people. The shepherd lost a sheep and searched for it. His act was appropriate for someone with his job; there is something heroic in his search for one sheep when ninety-nine were still back home. I value his perseverance, an attribute of God that should typify us as well. A woman lost a coin. She turned the house up-side-down to find it. I have heard scholars say she may have lost the coin she wore on her wedding headdress. It would have been precious, not just any coin. She searched for it in the same way we seek a lost wedding ring. But I wonder.

When I was in Israel, an elderly man gave us a coin from his collection. It was a Widow's mite, a coin from the story of a woman who gave all she had to the Temple treasury. (Luke 21:1-4) Jesus was watching everyone put in offering that day—the rich and the poor. She gave all she had—two tiny copper coins—Jesus said she gave more than anyone else, though the coins given by the rich would have been much heavier. I can fit my tiny Widow's mite on the end of my little finger and hardly know it is there. When I read the story of a woman searching for a lost coin, I wonder whether it was a mere mite. Was Jesus saying even the least among us is significant—another attribute of God's that should characterize the way we treat each other.

But that is not what caught my attention as I listened to the sermon that afternoon in chapel at the College where I teach. For the first time, I realized what it means to say people are different from coins and sheep. The woman and shepherd looked for objects that were waiting to be found—the sheep in a protected hollow in a hillock—a coin lying in some unlikely place until it occurred to a patient woman to look there. But the son; he is different. The father did not go out looking. He remained at home. Maybe he went on with business as usual, except that he kept one eye on the road to his front door. The son had to come to his senses. How does that happen? In meditating on loss and recovery, we must acknowledge the suffering we experience as we wait for someone we love to come home.

Jesus, I stand on the porch looking down the road.

I see no one coming. I fear I may go mad with waiting; my eyes burn

with looking. Helplessness presses my heart. If I close my eyes I can

see my loved one coming but when I open them, I am disappointed.

Help me hand this search over to you. Keep my heart from getting hard.

Let me believe you love the one I await even more than I do.

Let me see that you wait with me. Let me trust that you are out there

in a far country with the one I love. Show me the beauty outside my

front door. Let my vision be restored. You waited for me and now it is

my turn. But apart from you, I cannot wait with patient confidence for

the lost to return home. Let me see you standing with me.

Refresh my tired eyes.

Faith and Seeing

Jesus said, "For judgment I have come into this world, so that the blind will see and those who see will become blind." Some Pharisees who were with him heard him say this and asked, "What? Are we blind too?" Jesus said, "If you were blind, you would not be guilty of sin; but now that you claim you can see, your guilt remains."

John 9:39-41

Faith is being sure of what we hope for and certain of what we do not see.

Hebrews 11:1

Faith is not ordinary seeing. It requires a dependence on God like a blind person who needs a cane to get around. It is in this sense that faith depends on God. Faith is not blind, however. The faithful become skilled at perceiving the world in a way that is beyond ordinary vision—it is a way of seeing that appreciates the reality of God's presence in their lives. When it learns to see, faith influences human action due to the way it organizes our perception of reality. If we want to be well, we are compelled to make sense of life. Faithful seeing fills in gaps in our experience between what we can touch, taste, see, hear or smell and realities we cannot test empirically. Faith attends to depths that cannot be plumbed with a measuring stick. It makes connections between what can be and cannot be seen; it perceives reality beyond mere seeing. Faith as a way of seeing comes through practice in the company of faithful people. It is the capacity to see what is not yet visible and work for its realization with sustained and sustaining passion. Faith allows the materials at hand and people close by, to be part of the fabric of its final product. Faithful seeing is the heart's intellectual and spiritual work. Faithful seeing brings the intellect to bear on the problems of life. Scripture says, "We live by faith, not by sight." (2Corinthians 5:7)

Faith is a way of seeing the world. Vision gives us perspective, it lets us stand back to expand our view of a situation. What is seeing by faith? Seeing by faith is an aesthetic skill in the same way an artist sees a picture she will paint, realizing her vision on a finished canvas. Faith sees like an architect as he designs a building with paper and pencil. Faith sees like a gardener that observes her garden each year, confident that next year this plant or that shrub will be even more beautiful. Faith sees like an interior designer who knows what a room will look like when he is done even though rough materials clutter the room at present, or are not even purchased as yet. Seeing with eyes of faith is like a dress designer who takes shapeless material and sews it into garments that fit the body and soul of another woman.

But if we suffer loss, our vision is clouded by disappointment. We question our capacity to see at all. Surely, we were wrong to think God wanted us to marry that person, or to pray for a child we could never conceive. We shut our eyes due to the strain of looking for an answer to prayer. We are eye sore. Christ has compassion on those who want to see but whose vision is impaired by suffering losses that were too great for their souls to bear. Jesus understood another difficulty we have because we did not see him in historical time. He prayed "also for those who will believe in me through [the disciples] message....Father, I want those you have given me [all believers] to be with me where I am, and to see my glory, the glory you have given me before the creation of the world." (John 17:20; 24) There is a third sense of seeing and not seeing Jesus warned about. If we claim to see but our lives show no evidence of Christ, we are blind; we delude ourselves.

Lord, help me. Show me yourself and myself.

Let me see my own blindness. Show me how I am blinded by

refusing to open my eyes to evidence that does not support the way

I want the world to be. Awaken me. I know I cannot please you

without your help. (Hebrews 11:6) So I ask for your presence with me.

Come into this day with me—everywhere. Open my eyes and ears.

Faith and Hearing

Hear, O Israel: The Lord our God, the Lord
is one. Love the Lord your God with all your
heart and with all your soul and with all
your strength.

Deuteronomy 6:4-5

Those who have ears, let them hear.

Matthew 11:15

For this people's heart has become calloused;
they hardly hear with their ears, and they
have closed their eyes. Otherwise they
might see with their eyes, hear with their
ears, understand with their hearts and turn,
and I would heal them.

Matthew 13:15

If seeing allows us to stand back and get perspective on our situation, hearing gets us up close to God and each other. A friend told of his trip to the old city of Jerusalem. As he entered through the gate, he noticed a shepherd leading a line of sheep. He wondered how a shepherd got sheep to follow without getting lost in the city. Then he heard the shepherd speaking to a sheep closest to him. The sheep knew his voice, followed, and led others coming behind. Jesus spoke about a good shepherd and said, "I am the good shepherd; I know my sheep and my sheep know me—just as the Father knows me and I know the

Father." (John 10:3b;14-15a) Following Jesus comes by hearing; "faith comes from hearing the message, and the message is heard through the word of Christ." (Rom. 10:17)

Faith comes by hearing. Perhaps you recall a game in which a group of people passed a message by whispering it in the ear of a person next to them until the message traveled around the circle. The last person repeated the message and the group compared it with the original. It was funny to note the differences. What I hear is not the same as what you hear, though we listen to the same message. Hearing is uniquely psychological; it is risky, personal. It combines with assumptions about life, gathered and organized since childhood. We weave what we hear into what we have already learned through experience. What we hear affects us differently than what we see. We interiorize sound and build aspects of our identity as a result; we become what we believe we are hearing. If life continues as we expect, messages fit into assumptions we already have—until the shock of significant loss. If we lose something important, we question whether we were hearing right in the first place. We stop our ears and don't listen for God's voice, a voice we assumed we understood. We stand with hands over our ears, trying to keep out impressions we believe will only disappoint us because our confidence in God is shaken. At the same time, when we suffer, God's voice is the one thing we desperately long to hear.

Faith comes by hearing in another sense as well. Hearing is personal and communal. We hear together in community. In community, we are called to hear God, hear ourselves and hear one another—a complex task we often get wrong. We live with tension in what is heard personally and said communally, especially for those whose experience differs from the group. People draw near to hear one another and differences show up. Christ's incarnation has implications for our struggle to hear each other. He differed from us but came to be near us. He showed us how to be with others while being distinct from them. Christians can learn to hear one another despite their differences. But we must be patient.

Lord, I want to hear you speak. I want to faithfully represent to others the truth you convey to me. Help me speak of what I know of you, though I am not sure anyone listens. Help overcome my disappointment. Lord, please help me be patient with myself as I listen to you. Don't let me jump to conclusions. Help me wait with you, while listening. Help me consider what you are saying to me over time. In my anxiety, I have moved too quickly, reacted too strongly—to myself and other people. Help me calm down. Teach me to hear you.

Loss and Opposition

O Lord, how many are my foes! How many
rise up against me! Many are saying of me,
'God will not deliver him.'"

Psalm 3:1-2

Psalms of opposition are traditionally attributed to David. It is important to understand his social context to appreciate the novel way he dealt with problems of loss, recovery and conflict. In his world, all social relations were relations of power in which honour could be won or lost. Every encounter was a potential loss of honour. People defended themselves continuously. Only equals could play, but equals must play the game of honour and shame. Everyone was caught in a web of meaning-making based on winning or losing honour. Power relations were based on a fencing metaphor so life was like a sword fight. Yet, as a man after God's own heart, something a bit different is going on in David's psalms of opposition. Their characteristics include:

- A problem or request that is stated early
- A personal reference which expresses a distress that affects the poet directly
- An enemy is, or enemies are, causing David harm
- A view of God that assumes God is his helper
- No expression of doubt that God will help him
- The acknowledgement that God has not yet rescued David. He is waiting.

David saw that games of opposition were opportunities to practice freedom and not get trapped in them. For us as well, opposition helps to understand how power operates. All human beings exercise power by governing the behavior of others and and being governed by power exercised over them by others.

Opposition begins at birth. Infants have a capacity to govern the actions of others. Just put an infant in a group of adults and observe how the baby gets attention. The game of opposition also reveals our values; we only get caught by things we value. Some people try to dissolve the tension in opposition by refusing to live or to value anything. They think: If I want nothing, I cannot be disappointed. But Christianity is about life. Shutting down is not an option for us any more than it was for David. Personal happiness is a human good. It is a desire that everything should always go the way we would like it to; it is a sense of continuous well-being, enjoyment of life, complete satisfaction with one's condition. Opposition reveals to us what to value. Jesus engaged in opposition when Pharisees tried to trap him. In meeting their opposition, he taught us wisdom. Opposition is a testing ground for wisdom that comes from above, which is "first pure; then peaceable, gentle, willing to yield, full of mercy and good fruits, without a trace of partiality or hypocrisy." (James 3:17) Lord, I ask for the wisdom you give generously, without finding fault.

By examining David's experience we can learn to set appropriate boundaries. When someone opposes our happiness we mark off boundaries around our interests. Boundary maintaining is a normal human activity and every culture provides pre-arranged patterns to reduce the harm that one person may inflict on others. We can learn to identify cultural scripts that direct the setting of boundaries and compare them with Christian principles. Through opposition, rightly carried out, we learn to be like Jesus.

Have mercy, Lord. Teach me to set boundaries in the right places, places that please you. Help me become wise. Let me know what is good for me. Help me become aware of my desires that are God given and hold fast to them. Let me want what you want for me, Lord.

What Have I Done?

O Lord my God, if I have done this and
there is guilt on my hands—if I have done
evil to those who are at peace with me or
without cause have robbed my foes—then
let my enemies pursue and overtake me;
let them trample my life to the ground and
make me sleep in the dust.

Psalm 7:3-5

Sometimes we suffer from not knowing whether or how we have contributed to someone else's harm. David struggled with an idea that perhaps he caused someone pain. He was uncertain. Life is so complicated. We are entwined with other people. Our actions have some effects we did not foresee or intend. Still, we are accused of wrongdoing. We simply don't know if the accusation is fair. The accusation may come from friend or foe. David knew he had obligations to both: he could not hide from God an unjust action he had committed against his enemies. He lamented the possibility he might have hurt someone he loved as a friend. The singular feature of the psalm is that David is not hiding from God, even though he is not entirely sure whether he is guilty. He seemed to believe he was innocent but in contrast to the confidence he expressed in other psalms, he was uneasy. Perhaps the person or people accusing him had good evidence on their side. God must judge. The psalm is a testament to his trust in God's fairness: "O righteous God, who searches minds and hearts, bring to an end the violence of the wicked and make the righteous secure." (Psalm 7:9) In the psalm we see a man who is uncertain how to judge his own action but still willing to stand before God as his judge.

There are at least two ways in which this psalm might be a dangerous prayer. He may have been guilty and soon there would be evidence to prove it and confirmation from God that he did what was evil. Yet he uttered the words before God that his enemies should pursue him to death for what he did. Is he serious? David was a passionate poet. His righteousness is revealed by his trust in God, whether or not he was actually guilty. The psalm speaks of confidence in God even if he was uncertain about himself. As a man after God's own heart, he was willing to bring his offence before the Holy One. His willingness to question himself before God says a great deal. But what if his prayer is mere bravado? What if he was hiding from responsibility for action that hurt someone else? What if he was blind to sin? Why should we hear authenticity in his prayer?

I think we should trust its honest self-searching and truth-telling because elsewhere David took responsibility for wrongdoing. This psalm invites us to use the occasions when we are blamed or accused as an opportunity for authentic self-assessment before Almighty God—who knows and sees the truth about us. Yes, we are capable of and do hurt other people. Yet, even though we sin, we are welcome to come before God and ask to be forgiven. Our value to God is not erased by the sin we commit. David was sure of this truth. The psalm is an invitation to stand before God and ask him to search our hearts and reveal the truth for all to see. It is an act of courage based in fearlessness before the truth. David revealed a truth for us all: to be judged by God is good. If we are guilty, we can be forgiven. If innocent, we can be restored. David brought his confusion to God and found comfort. Likewise, we come before God with events that trouble the heart and threaten our happiness. We stand up before God unafraid.

Lord, here I am. Speak truth to me. I have seen what happens when people turn away from hearing the truth from you. Don't let me be someone who lives under a false impression that I can do no wrong. Almighty God, help me. Let me see that there is more to me than this one event in which I struggle to get clear about my role in the pain someone else is feeling. Uncloud my vision. Please, let me see you.

My Righteous Plea

> As for what others do—by the word of your
> lips I have kept myself from the ways of the
> violent. My steps have held to your paths;
> my feet have not slipped.
>
> **Psalm 17:4-5**

We live in a modern world focused on guilt—white guilt, male guilt, mother guilt, childhood guilt. Somewhere, somehow, everything bad is connected to what we did or shouldn't have done. We drown in guilt due to responsibility we sense, even for things happening very far away. The psalmist did not see the world this way. Psalm 17 expresses innocence, a righteousness alien to the Western mind. His assurance is available to us at the beginning of this century since we are in the midst of a major critique of modern consciousness. Part of that critique questions whether it is right to feel guilty for everything. Modern folk were guilt-ridden. But modern guilt did not make people better, kinder, less racist. It hardened the heart to the possibility of being genuinely good. Real guilt is meant to lead us toward repentance, not to a swamp of unrelenting self-abuse.

David perceived his own righteousness and relied on that assurance. He knew that God saw and heard every action he took or refrained from taking, every word he uttered or withheld. God's knowledge of humanity is manifest in the intimacy of Psalm 139: "O

Lord, you have searched me and you know me. You know when I sit and when I rise...you are familiar with all my ways. Before a word is on my tongue you know it completely, O Lord." (Psalm 139:1-4) Are you at ease with knowing that God sees you with clear vision? Becoming comfortable with being seen by God is part of growing up as a person of faith. The confidence expressed in the psalm is remarkable: "Though you probe my heart and examine me at night, though you test me, you will find nothing; I have resolved that my mouth will not sin." (Psalm 17:3) Perhaps, because he was not swimming in a culture of guilt, he had confidence to let God examine his heart. Here I am, Lord. Come and look at your servant. I have done nothing wrong! There is nothing to hide.

As you reflect on the psalm, I invite you to consider that sometimes you are innocent of wrong when bad things happen. How can we be sure that suffering sometimes has nothing to do with sin we committed? I want to be clear that I refer to sin committed intentionally or inadvertently that has brought about suffering like that conveyed in Psalm 17: "my mortal enemies surround me. They close up their callous hearts; their mouths speak with arrogance. They have tracked me down; they now surround me, with eyes alert to throw me to the ground. They are like a lion hungry for prey, like a great lion crouching in cover." (Psalm 17:9b-12) In coming to understand righteousness, we learn to distinguish among the feelings of shame, sorrow and guilt.

David was aware of the harm his enemies caused him. He was not paranoid, as we accuse people now, dismissing a very painful aspect of suffering and loss. He was in pain because of the way people were treating him. He was not imagining looks on people's faces—the way their backs turned toward him as he entered a room. He felt the shunning, the hardening of their gaze—he knew they were against him. There are times when those around us turn away through no fault of ours. If this happens, we find refuge in Psalm 17. We cry out in innocence and ask God to come to our aid. We grasp the commitment to remain righteous, regardless of present suffering. God sees us. We choose not to retaliate. We did not sin in the first place; we will not sin now due to pressure we feel from unjust judgment. We remain faithful and cry out to God.

O Lord, please relieve my shame. I am drowning in sorrow, not guilt.

Walk with me into rooms of people that no longer respect me—whose

eyes are sharp and piercing. Rescue me. Help me endure.

My God,

   my God,

      why have you forsaken me?

Psalm 22:1

Jesus was hanging on the cross when he uttered the first words of this psalm. He suffered and died that we might have life, eternal life—knowing God and Jesus Christ, whom God sent. How does his cry from the cross show us the nature of God? What can we learn if we have the courage to observe Jesus hanging there and acknowledge that our sin nailed him to that tree? We can see that our suffering is situated within his suffering. Our suffering makes sense because he suffered, bled, died—and rose again to new life! This is the story of the cross—that we can be free to live and to suffer in his name. How do we do that? It takes a life of love to answer that question.

What was David going through when he wrote these words? The psalm directs the reader's gaze in several places as its author moved through his experience and settled on a point of view at the end. Where does the psalmist invite us to look? He looked first at despair: "Why are you so far from saving me, so far from the words of my groaning? O my God, I cry out by day, but you do not answer, by night, and I am not silent." (Psalm 22:1-2) His pain is boundless. Is God absent, unseeing and unhearing—so unlike the God he thought he knew? So the psalmist looked back to the history of his people. He recalled God's Holiness and remembered a day when his ancestors called out to God who heard their cry and delivered them. Remembering brings him no comfort, only a question: Why is God absent from me now then? He decided he must be worthless: "I am a worm and not a human being, scorned by everyone and despised by the people. All who see me mock me; they hurl insults, shaking their heads, they say "he trusts in the Lord; let the Lord rescue him. Let him deliver him, since he delights in him." (Psalm 22:6-8) That was his feeling: it was not the truth. Suffering assaults the value we put on ourselves—a value we thought other people placed on us as well. Humanity is fragile and is damaged when we are misunderstood or misrecognized. We are not the solitary, strong supermen Western society held up as the human ideal. We feel weak, like worms.

The honour and shame system that shaped the psalmist's culture was very clear: in the absence of recognition from others, a solitary person had no value. In the twentieth century we talked ourselves into thinking that we were above this social limitation—a need for recognition. We came to believe in dignity, not honour. We believed an individual's value is certain if he affirms it by himself. Suffering teaches a different lesson: modernity did not secure individual human value—we are also what we are perceived as by others—except that is, in God's economy. The psalmist holds on to his value before God, even though from that safe perch he could see strong bulls of Bashan encircling him, roaring lions surrounding him, dogs snapping at his heels.

His circumstances overwhelmed him; history did not encourage him and he turned his gaze to a third place—the point of view of faith. In the psalms of opposition there is a faith perspective that holds sure: God will come to our aid. God has not yet come, but will. Faith turned

David's gaze to the future. Despite suffering, we can still look to the future. We can ask ourselves what we want our situation to be like two years from now, two months from now, two minutes from now. What are we prepared to do to help a good future come about? Suffering knocks us off balance; leaves us dazed and reeling. Hold fast to your gaze on God as a focal point to bring you upright again.

Lord Jesus, let me see you clearly so I can be steady and stand secure.

I will stay in your presence and not be moved by the racket around me,

with your help.

Remember Me Well

Remember not the sins of my youth and my
rebellious ways; according to your love
remember me, for you are good, O Lord.

Psalm 25:7

A tree was removed from a courtyard where I work. Everyone was sad. It was planted when the College was built. It was old, outwardly beautiful but rotten to its core. It had to go. I stood at my window and gazed at its outer beauty concealing inner decay. "Lord," I prayed: "Please root out everything in me that is dying. It's time!" I had no idea of the transformation awaiting me. When something is dead at its heart, we cannot name it but we feel distant, dissatisfied and fearful. It is the feeling children have as they play a game of hide and seek; they are terrified of being found but can't stay in the game if they are not caught. To have healthy fear of God is different from an isolating fear of other people. If we invite God to remove what is dead inside us, we look toward a future that can deal with fear. Loving the past is important to recovery. Can we do it? Are we tempted to diminish sins that haunt our history? Do we minimize them and pretend they did not happen? Are we hiding? I love a quotation from John Dewey when I am tempted to lie about my past. He said people that are fully alive make peace with the past, even their own stupidity and see the future, not as ominous, but full of promise. The past links to the future as we experience the present. If we love the past, we relax in the present and see the future as hopeful. To love the past is to tell the truth.

David acknowledged his sin. He struggled to feel confident but knew coming before the Lord was his only way forward: "For the sake of your name, O Lord, forgive my iniquity, though it is great." (Psalm 25:11) Why does he say, for the sake of your name? Hidden sin produces rottenness in one way or another. When we hide sin or lie about it, God's name is dishonoured. Small shoots spring up in the words we use to hurt and insult other people—in jealousy, anger, resentment. Rottenness does not go unnoticed forever, even if a tree produces green leaves each spring. We continually feel fearful and need to lie. We recoil from embarrassing surprises unless we make peace with who we really are; a false self is an unstable identity. If you are a leader, lying is dangerous. You have one path open to freedom and relief: "Good and upright is the Lord; therefore he instructs sinners in his ways. He guides the humble in what is right and teaches them his way." (Psalm 25:8-9) Would you like to feel free? If you keep sin in your heart and refuse to let God root it out, you are unable to see and hear the Living God. You will work relentlessly to be productive and feel tired; but you will not conceal the decay. Jesus saw: "For this people's heart has grown dull, and their ears are hard of hearing, and they have shut their eyes; so that they might not look with their eyes, and listen with their ears, and understand with their heart and turn—and I would heal them." (Matthew 13:15)

Healing comes as we see and hear God; it arrives as a gift. In accepting the gift we perceive what is going on in our hearts: we hear the fear that motivates insults we throw at others. Fear isolates us; we turn away from those who could help until we are driven away in loneliness. Lying about ourselves is a barrier to relationship and eventually means being deaf to God. Scripture says, "The Lord confides in those who fear him; he makes his covenant known to them." (Psalm 25:14) Are you listening? Can you see? How can we perceive our own sin if we are hiding from it at the same time? We only see by listening—to God and those we love who are trying to tell us they want to be close but approaching us is painful. Can you let God love you, as you remember who you really are?

Come near me, Lord Jesus. Calm my heart.

Open my eyes. Quiet my fear.

Here I Stand

Vindicate me, O Lord, for I have led a
blameless life; I have trusted in the Lord
without wavering.

Psalm 26:1

In Jewish and Christian tradition, the author of the psalms of opposition is thought to be David—a shepherd, King and a man after God's
own heart. These psalms have commonalities: they are personal
assurances that God will rescue David from something that has gone
terribly wrong, but God has not yet come to his aid. But if this psalm
was written by David, how could he stand before God to be examined
when we know from his life that he did sin? Why does he say he led
a blameless life? The answer is important. I hope it is one you ask
about your own life. In psalm 26, David expressed himself honestly
and believed God saw him completely. How could he do both? How
could he say he led a blameless life, when in other psalms he asked
forgiveness for sins of his youth, or actions he carried out that harmed
other people and offended God? In psalm 32, also attributed to David,
he spoke as a sinner and said, "When I kept silent, my bones wasted
away though my groaning all day long....Then I acknowledged my sin
to you and did not cover up my iniquity....and you forgave the guilt of
my sin." (Psalm 32:3-5) What is going on? What can we learn from

David about losing and recovering ourselves?

Perhaps these psalms were written at different times—at the beginning he was blameless and at the end he realized he had sinned. Maybe that is why they appear contradictory when we hold them up together. David claims at different times that he was sinful and blameless before God. Yet if the lifespan answer is the right one, wouldn't he be inclined to get rid of poems that were contradictory? Wouldn't he sort through them and present a coherent picture of his life, as either a sinner or as a saint but not as both? I am tempted to do that. I think we are all tempted to tell a story of our lives that makes us out to be either hopeless sinners that can't change, or as worthy saints that must keep others at a distance. Christianity teaches we are sinners and saints. How do you hold these two truths in tension in your own life?

We get guidance from David if we recognize coherence in his life story. In poetry directed toward God, for the benefit of believers, he recounted depths of experience. He suffered loss and recovered from it, although we know his sin exacted payment as well, despite his acceptance that he was forgiven. The child died that he fathered with Bathsheba, to his great grief. In moving from loss to recovery, David held firm to his love for God. He knew the only loss he could not endure was the loss of God. Every other loss was bearable, even if he mourned it deeply. In order to walk a blameless life, David took responsibility for his actions; he spoke as someone who could control himself: "I do not sit with the deceitful, nor do I consort with hypocrites; I abhor the assembly of evildoers and refuse to sit with the wicked....I love the house where you live, O Lord, the place where your glory dwells." (Psalm 26:4-5) He held himself accountable and allowed God free access to his heart. Do you? When he sinned, David let God's forgiveness cleanse him completely. Like Jesus washing the disciples' feet, he permitted God to free him from the guilt of his sin.

Will you? The coherence in his life holds together because he kept no record of his wrongs. He believed God kept no record of his wrongs. So he was able to tell God the truth about himself, eventually—if not right away.

Lord, help me to stop hiding. Let me come out into the Light of your presence, into your forgiveness. Let me stand tall in your presence as I acknowledge my weakness and the tendencies that create trouble, for me and others. I want to be accountable in your presence. Help me trust that I can change. Let me know that you love me.

Broken Pottery

Because of all my enemies, I am the utter
contempt of my neighbors; I am a dread to
my friends—those who see me in the street
flee from me. I am forgotten by them as
though I were dead; I have become like
broken pottery.

Psalm 31:11-12

Twentieth century popular psychology did an injustice to human suffering. We all know about paranoia and sense a reproach grow whenever someone confesses they feel that no one likes them. Right, we think, well, you are just paranoid. Get over it. Our response to loss and suffering is inhumane. It is an ignorant reaction for two reasons that psalms of opposition reveal. First, if we gain enemies, we lose friends. That was the psalmist's experience; he knew it to be the case. He could see his neighbors and friends turn away from him due to the suspicion surrounding him on every side. Shunning goes along with suffering as a sociological reality—we are not confused or mistaken. As the poet points out—friends literally turn away from us though we need them desperately. Secondly, shunning is an element of the suffering itself. Where there is smoke, there must be fire, as the saying goes. If we are in trouble, we must have deserved it in some way or it wouldn't have happened. Suspicion grows like cancer; we are caught in its aggression. When we are distressed due to gains made by those who oppress us intentionally, we suffer the loss of support from people who used to provide it. In our suffering, we are drawn forcefully down into mire that frustrates any attempt to rectify the initial causes of our trouble.

In this psalm, David described himself as a besieged city—an amazing metaphor. A city beset by enemies on every side is also cut off from friends and neighboring towns. The siege is effective because those inside are cut off from food, water, weapons and ammunition. A town must exist on resources it stocked up in good times. Those inside the city watch supplies dwindle with no help on the horizon. Shunning is a subtle sociological pattern that comes into play when we are besieged by others. People will expend energy to ensure no one comes to our aid, through whispering, gossip and aggression as well as through subtle embodied language that shuffles its feet when we speak, scoffs at, or minimizes our complaints and worry. What we have learned to call paranoia is a justifiable sensibility that recognizes we are alone in a besieged city. The good news is that Jesus experienced and understood the feeling of utter isolation.

As for the psalmist, he turned to God: "But I trust in you, O Lord; I say, 'You are my God'. My times are in your hands; deliver me from my enemies and from those who pursue me. Let your face shine on your servant; save me in your unfailing love. Let me not be put to shame, O Lord, for I have cried out to you." (Psalm 31:14-17a) The poet was right to see in God an eternal and inexhaustible source of strength. Resources replenished by God never run out. Yet Jesus added an insight essential to Christian community. Support, like forgiveness, must be both human and divine in order to rescue us from isolation and despair. In short, someone needs to believe in us. Without support from others, we are locked in trouble that occurred at one point in time but continues to glue our feet to the ground. Given the humiliation of being stuck, it is hard to ask for help. It is hard to cry out if we feel we are also cut off from God's sight. Yet crying out is a first step to finding resources to live on until the siege ceases and we move freely once again. In the midst of suffering, surrender your vain attempts to provision yourself out of a storehouse that is fast depleting in its stock of goods. Realize your poverty and cry out:

Lord, help me. How great is your goodness stored up for those who fear you, which you bestow in the sight of all who take refuge in you. Lord Jesus, I can no longer defend myself. Help me stop pretending with you.

I Would Never Do This To You!

Ruthless witnesses...question me on things
I know nothing about. They repay me evil
for good and leave my soul forlorn. Yet
when they were ill, I put on sackcloth and
humbled myself with fasting. When my
prayers returned to me unanswered, I
went about mourning as though for my
friend or brother. I bowed my head in
grief as though weeping for my mother. But
when I stumbled, they gathered in glee...
They slandered me without ceasing.

Psalm 35:11-14

Loss and suffering have a remarkable tendency to draw us downward in spirals that seem never-ending. An emotional shock accompanying loss is the absence of compassion from others based on what we could call relational amnesia. Could the poet's enemies not remember how he treated them when they were ill? Pain goes very deep when we see people treating us in ways we have never treated them. We are shunned, though we have offered them care. How can we address the hurt and humiliation? We become invisible. Good things we have done in the past are forgotten.

A young psychologist was discussing his practice with me in general terms and noted a pattern he thought was remarkable: when they are in conflict, married people tell a story about their relationship that denies they were ever in love. One begins to reject and withdraw from the other and tells a story that supports the move away. My friend finds this interesting. In his work, he tries to help them remember what first drew them together. Sometimes he is successful—or I should say—they are successful at recalling that they loved each other once, for good reasons.

This psalm acknowledges the depth of our loss when we are ganged up on, as it were. David felt the disdain of a gloating crowd who were glad to keep their distance from him. It is as though ordinary, unreflective people believe that suffering and loss are somehow contagious. They must keep their distance and assure friends and acquaintances that the sufferer is not like them. In the book of Job, the suffering Job describes with precision the effects in his body of the rejection he felt from people that he used to treat generously. (Job 19) In the New Testament, the treatment of lepers is not unlike the patterns of behaviour people demonstrate toward one who suffers. What are those of us to do who have felt others turn away in a time of need? Often Job's friends are criticized for beliefs they upheld that tested Job's patience. But as harsh as their words seem, they did not leave or turn away. They remained, though they did not realize what was happening to him; for their faithfulness, they are to be congratulated and forgiven for their lack of insight.

The psalmist's honesty is refreshing. He hated those who turned away from him. But in anger, he did not carry out vengeance. His restraint was not necessarily commendable; perhaps he showed restraint because he really had nothing powerful enough in his arsenal to use effectively. When we are low, we often have no resources left to carry out revenge. Our devalued state keeps us from retribution. We feel so small—anything we try to say or do only brings scorn from those who shun us. Perhaps it is in this low state that we finally turn to the One whose resources never run out. The psalmist cries out for protection from unbearable shame. Throughout the psalms of opposition, David identified crushing despair and humiliation that arose as a result of suffering. He called out for God to cover the naked exposure he could not escape. He cried, "O Lord, you have seen this; be not silent. Do not be far from me, O Lord. Awake, and rise to my defence! Contend for me, my God and my Lord." (Psalm 35:22-23)

Lord, you see me. You recognize me. You remember the good

that I did to others, even if they refuse to recall who I am.

Let me know with assurance that my value to you is sufficient to

sustain me for the time being. Let me know of your love. Please, Lord

Jesus, strengthen my courage, for I am weak, worried and weary.

They Love to Sin

An oracle is within my heart concerning
the sinfulness of the wicked: There is no
fear of God before their eyes. For in their
own eyes they flatter themselves too much
to detect or hate their sin. The words of
their mouths are wicked and deceitful;
they have ceased to be wise and to do
good. Even on their beds they plot evil;
they commit themselves to a sinful course
and do not reject what is wrong.

Psalm 36:1-4

There is a theme running through psalms of opposition that the poet summarized in Psalm 36. It is an insight that allowed him to endure suffering, to stay the course, to continue placing trust in God, even though God had not yet rescued him. The insight turned his attention away from fear and despair that entangled him and could trip him up. It is an insight that prevented him from drowning in self-absorption, though I do not say this to deny his need to pay attention to the feel of his suffering. For it was in paying careful attention to his inner struggle that insights came, as a gift from God. Insight arrived because he did not turn away from his own pain. In seeing his suffering, he realized how evil operates in the hearts of those who refuse to do the right thing.

Pain is interesting. My niece is a massage therapist and has learned a lot about the body and its habits. Because she constantly works on people, she is often in pain due to the way she uses her hands and arms in therapeutic massage. Once I came to her with a pain in my thumb that nothing would ease. She massaged it for a while, which helped, but gave me an insight that helped even more. She asked me to focus on the pain in my hand. Was it a sharp pain? Was it diffused pain? Did it move? Where was it exactly? When did I feel it? When did it start? Is it always the same? What made it worse? She asked me to sit quietly and answer the questions. She experienced so much pain that she started asking herself these questions. She told me that once she attended to her pain she realized it moved; if she focused on it, she realized it shifted and changed. Once she realized pain moves, it was easier to believe that she would be relieved eventually. She said that when people are in physical pain, they often turn away from it and try to ignore it. They tense up the muscles around the sore area, making the pain worse. Trying to ignore physical pain locks it on, so to speak. Emotional pain is not entirely different.

The psalmist did not underestimate his suffering. But through reflection, he perceived how evil operates in another human heart. He acknowledged he was a sinner but saw a difference between being a sinner himself and people who focused energy on harming others. People committed to evil flatter themselves and think that God cannot see what they are doing. They set up their own view of the world as a standard for behaviour because they believe they are smarter than God. They may claim to be Christian but if you listen and observe, you sense that, at best, God annoys them. He is in their way. There is little that persuades them of the wrong inherent in their actions. They take pleasure in causing pain; lying is their way of life. In response to evil people, David did two things: he identified his own pain and its effects on him and he focused on God. Yes, some people are dedicated to evil. Yes, God is love. He realized that, "Your love, O Lord, reaches to the heavens, your faithfulness to the skies. Your righteousness is like the mighty mountains, your justice like the great deep. O Lord, you preserve both people and animals. How precious is your unfailing love! Both highborn and low find refuge in the shadow of your wings. They feast in the abundance of your house; you give them drink from your river of delights. For with you is the fountain of life; in your light we see light." (Psalm 36:5-9) The light of the world sheds light on our suffering.

Thank you God, for giving us Jesus so we can see what is going on.

Flee Revenge!

Do not fret because of those who are evil
or be envious of those who do wrong; for
like the grass they will soon wither, like
green plants they will soon die away. Trust
in the Lord and do good; dwell in the land
and enjoy safe pasture. Delight yourself in
the Lord and he will give you the desires of
your heart. Commit your way to the Lord;
trust in him and he will do this: He will
make your righteousness shine like the
dawn, the justice of your cause like the
noonday sun.

Psalm 37:1-6

There is no greater struggle for those who suffer than to resist a temptation to become what they hate in others. Under normal circumstances, we copy what others have done to us and pass it on. The best way to understand someone who hurts you is to realize they likely have been hurt in the same way they create havoc in your life. What to do? The psalmist offers an unlikely scenario: pay attention to yourself; trust God. It may seem impossible to ask those who are drowning in loss to trust God for the desires of their heart, yet it is the remarkable promise of Psalm 37.

When wronged, by parents, spouses or friends, we plot revenge and focus our thought on how to pay them back. We incessantly review all they have done. Like CNN, we run tapes over and over and over mentally. We stand Jesus' instruction on its head. He asked us to love others the way we want to be loved. Instead, we love them like they love us—blow for blow, insult for insult—or we wish we could. We want to hurt them the way they hurt us. It is essential for recovery to force attention away from the tape that keeps playing revenge. But the psalmist did not suddenly feel warmth toward those who hurt him. Rather, he comforted himself that wickedness repays its own price: "The wicked draw the sword and bend the bow to bring down the poor and needy, to slay those who are upright. But their swords will pierce their own hearts, and their bows will be broken." (Psalm 37: 14-15) He shared this insight, not to gloat over their demise but to help himself turn off that internal tape that enslaves our attention. He regained a right feeling about wickedness so that he would not be drawn into its deathtrap. And he trusted God. Trust is found by balancing a value we put on ourselves, feeling the strain of our suffering, and resting in God. As we learn balance, trust eventually takes root in the heart. The poet urged himself and us to "be still before the Lord and wait patiently for him: do not fret when people succeed in their ways; when they carry out their wicked schemes. Refrain from anger and turn from wrath; do not fret—it leads only to evil." (Psalm 37:7-8)

The psalmist is resolute. He will not take revenge. God will protect, console, set things right. But confidence in God to defend us is precisely what is so hard to trust if we are lost in humiliation. It is an act of the will to trust God when we suffer. As we turn attention to the characteristics of God, we seek out the righteous as our examples. The psalmist observed, "I have seen the wicked and ruthless flourishing like a green tree in its native soil, but they soon passed away and were no more; though I looked for them, they could not be found. Consider the blameless, observe the upright; there is a future for those who seek peace." (Psalm 37:35-37) In confidence, we stand tall in the presence of our enemies. God is the lifter of our heads. We do not pursue revenge; we value ourselves as God's beloved. If God is for us, who can stand against us?

> *Lord, you came to earth to show us how to suffer*
>
> *and remain resolute in your love, show me how to live.*
>
> *My anger is not diminished but please don't let me sin*
>
> *against others the way they have they sinned*
>
> *against me. Not that I am a better person, Lord,*
>
> *but simply because you have shown me my sin.*
>
> *I see it.*

Cornered by Suffering

Sacrifice and offering you did not desire,
but my ears you have pierced; burnt
offerings and sin offerings you did not
require. Then I said, 'Here I am, I have
come—it is written about me in the scroll.
I desire to do your will, O my God; your
law is written within my heart.

Psalm 40:6-8

The psalmist was suffering due to his own sin: "For troubles without number surround me; my sins have overtaken me, and I cannot see. They are more than the hairs of my head, and my heart fails within me. Be pleased, O Lord, to save me; O Lord, come quickly to help me. May all who seek to take my life be put to shame and confusion; may all who desire my ruin be turned back in disgrace." (Psalm 40:12-14) We are sometimes sure of things that seem contradictory. Psalm 40 is rich with contrary feelings. David was sure God had turned to rescue him. He was aware he stood on a solid rock God provided as a safe place for his feet. He was willing to speak boldly to others about the salvation of the Lord. Yet he was afraid and sensed a need for God's protection and asked for mercy. He knew he was guilty. He knew he was blessed. He knew he was poor and wanted help. He was waiting. He knew he had help already. How can apparently contradictory feelings co-exist in the human heart? Believers live in many dimensions of time synchronously: past, present and future. We gather all these times in our hearts and rely on them when suffering. In God's presence, David had available the full resources of time and eternity.

If spiritual rebellion is the refusal to hear and see, Psalm 40 is a moment of complete surrender. In contrast to freedom to move among past, present and future times, suffering traps us in a one-time event. Time moves slowly; it seems unending. But a moment of surrender is the beginning of release. Freedom comes as we tell God the truth, despite the confusion we feel. God forgives us. As Hannah Arendt understood,

> without being forgiven, released from the consequences of what we have done, our capacity to act would…be confined to one single deed from which we could never recover; we would remain the victims of its consequences forever, not unlike the sorcerer's apprentice who lacked the magic formula to break the spell.[9]

Arendt pointed out that Jesus understood that we need others to forgive us so we can feel assured of God's forgiveness.

David did not enjoy support from the people that surrounded him. Some delighted in his losses. So he turned to God for consolation. He saw that two strong ideas are true simultaneously: We need others; we only need God. These are two of the hard rocks of contrary feeling the soul may crash upon in the midst of a storm of suffering. Learn to navigate between them, keeping both in sight so as not to wreck yourselves on either one. Contradiction is an opportunity to let God show us how to steer between extremes that terrify us at the present time.

Lord, I bring you a mess of contradictory feelings that are in

my heart right now. They make no sense. Here I am. I am a sinner,

yet I stand with my head held high in your presence—that makes

no sense. I have wronged you but I offer to be your witness—that makes no sense. I ask you to protect me from other people, though I deserve to be punished for what I have done—that makes no sense. Holy and heavenly Father, accept the mess I am offering you. Thank you for piercing my ears so I hear you say I can come to you even with disorder in my soul. My need for you is very great. You are greater than my need. Your purposes are more significant than my sin. I will not let my sin matter more than you. Accomplish your will in me, just as I am, without one plea but that your love has rescued me. You know everything about me. I am sorry for what I have done. I am standing at the helm of my ship and ask you to lead me through these deep waters.

Everyone Conspires

All my enemies whisper together against
me; they imagine the worst for me, saying,
'A vile disease has beset him; he will never
get up from the place where he lies'. Even
my close friend, whom I trusted, he who
shared my bread, has lifted up his heel
against me.

Psalm 41:7-9

Years ago, a young girl was abducted in Winnipeg and was missing for six weeks. The city searched for her. She was found dead in a construction shed. She died of exposure the day before she was found. I heard about the search though I lived two provinces away. Years later, I met her mother at a conference. In conversing with her, we began to count up bits and pieces of evil that the young girl's abduction unleashed in her friends and acquaintances. Harm caused by the man who abducted her eventually rippled through my own life story.

I used to dislike the idea David expressed in this poem that when he sinned, he sinned against God only. If we think of the wrong he committed against Bathsheba and Uriah, wasn't his action primarily against a woman, her husband, and their families? Why did he focus on God as the injured party? More recently, the idea we sin primarily against God became important to me. The psalmist is right to say that we sin against God mainly. The world suffers ruinous harm if a little girl dies at the hands of one who is morally lost. Recently, twenty-three years later, he has been found through DNA evidence. But the hurt he caused cannot be healed even by his conviction.

When we sin, God's beloved creation is harmed. With every sin, the world has more disease in it. God's work gets harder. Recall that David distinguished between those committed to evil and those like himself that loved God but continued to do what is foolish and wrong, inadvertently or by design. Should we be eager to make a distinction between sinners and evil people? I think we are well advised to do so since it is the hardening of the heart that creates distance between us and God. Sin can be forgiven—relationships with God can be restored. But the world is different than it was before we sinned. We are forgiven, but the world has more to deal with—unending difficulty we do not calculate in advance or know how to measure once sin is set loose in the world. Our hearts become entirely hardened to the effects of sin if we commit ourselves to evil.

In the psalm, the poet is ill, on a bed of suffering. He pleaded, 'O, Lord, have mercy on me; heal me, for I have sinned against you.' (Psalm 41:4) He may have thought his illness occurred due to what he did wrong. That belief is not only ancient. I recall the reaction of someone close to me when I was diagnosed with a disease for which there is no cure.[10] This person wondered out loud what I had done wrong to deserve the sickness. She could think of some things, given time. Since she wasn't sick, did that imply she was sinless? David's illness was worsened by people around him. Those who surrounded him went much further than my family member. They gloated over his illness and potential demise. They cheered on his hardship, hoping it would win over him! How could this be? He observed, "My enemies say of me in malice, 'When will he die and his name perish?' Whenever they come to see me, they speak falsely, while their hearts slander; then they go out and spread it abroad." (Psalm 41:5-6) He brought his confusion to God: did I sin? If so, it was against you. Please heal me. He reminded God of his integrity. Unlike the person who abducted that little girl, David was trapped inside an incident he may have brought on himself, he wasn't sure, but whose effects he could not ignore. He asked for mercy and reassurance.

Lord Jesus Christ, have mercy on me. Let me not hold malice

in my heart toward those who conspire against me. Restore me

to full fellowship with you, even as I am in distress.

Even Strangers Attack Me!

Strangers are attacking me; ruthless people
seek my life—people without regard for
God. Surely God is my help; the Lord is the
one who sustains me.

Psalm 54:3-4

Pursuit is a common theme in the psalms when opposition assumes an extreme form. We often want to run and hide in response to trouble. If we examine all thirty psalms we can map the rich texture of a life that met with opposition from enemies, strangers and friends. It is remarkable that the psalmist was so free to express feelings that came along with trials he faced. He was not afraid of God. Since the chase at times was literal, he hid from people but not from God. The poet told God that he was being pursued and attacked; he ran and hid but in the midst of his fear, he was honest with God.

The struggle to resist a desire to run and hide is complicated by our need to be believed. Living with opposition teaches us that those who run and hide lose their credibility. The internal conflict emphasizes the need to be believed, to have a witness to our suffering. David said, "Let evil recoil on those who slander me; in your faithfulness destroy them." (Psalm 54:5) Perhaps you've had the displeasure of sitting in a meeting, designed as a chance for reconciliation that became an opportunity for your enemy to attack you again, even accusing you of his or her own crime. Such accusations go deep and sting profoundly when spoken in front of people who have no way of knowing who is telling the truth. Rage mixes with the absurdity of what is happening—a mix of feelings captured by the familiar expression that we don't know whether to laugh or cry.

How can you defend yourself? You cannot stand up to accusations if they do not conform to a typical way we resolve questions of who is telling the truth. We rely on witnesses to support one person against the other. We need a third party to declare who is and who is not telling the truth. But so many of the offences we suffer have no witnesses. They are events that take place between two people with no one else there—no one saw—there is no one to judge justly. The need to be believed is at the heart of suffering. We endure many things, but the isolation of having neither witness nor credibility is destructive to human identity. In my experience it is often those that lie who sound most convincing. They have thought long and hard about how to defend themselves. They have practice and a purpose. Innocent people are incoherent, confused, astonished by what is going on. They are caught off guard and are unprepared with a response. To those who suffer in this way, some of the rules they counted on have been violated. They are in shock and cannot collect themselves when questioned. Their side of the story does not come off well in front of people that try to judge what happened. These judges need to know what David understood and revealed in the psalms about those who do evil. David understood how futile defending one's self can be when there are no witnesses and when it is hard to believe those who claim they have been oppressed. David descried the ruthlessness of his enemies. He trusted God and tried to learn wisdom; he perceived patterns in how people act so he could decode behavior.

Wisdom is a science as well as an art. Those who suffer have opportunities to learn wisdom. It is hard to get; we receive it from God by being good observers of humanity.

Lord Jesus, if you are offering me wisdom from above, let me perceive and accept it—it is not an easy gift to receive—it always comes the hard way. Help me open my hands to treasure it in my heart. Thank you for knowing me and seeing me. Let be open with you. Let your wisdom guide my life, Lord Jesus.

Just Run Away!

My heart is in anguish within me; the terrors
of death assail me. Fear and trembling have
beset me; horror has overwhelmed me.
I said, "Oh, that I had the wings of a dove!
I would fly away and be at rest—I would
flee far away and stay in the desert;
I would hurry to my place of shelter,
far from the tempest and the storm.

Psalm 55:4-8

Running away sounds so attractive. While I was going through a particularly difficult time, I would get on my bicycle and ride to the next town, a round trip of about seventy kilometers. I am not athletic but felt desperate to escape. I had so many entanglements; literally to run away didn't appear possible. Reading the psalms is an escape in a different sense—a way out by going farther in. This psalm names a situation we may find ourselves in: "My companion attacks his friends; he violates his covenant. His speech is smooth as butter, yet war is in his heart; his words are more soothing than oil, yet they are drawn swords." (Psalm 55:20-21) There are many kinds of suffering: physical, relational, emotional. Another kind is what I call epistemological suffering—a word that has to do with how we know anything at all. This kind of suffering occurs when we cannot make sense of what is going on. We endure physical or emotional injury with patience but remain unable to make sense of why someone acts hurtfully, especially when it offers him or her no advantage. David lamented, "if an enemy were insulting me, I could endure it; if a foe were rising against me, I could hide. But it is you, one like myself, my companion, my close friend, with whom I enjoyed sweet fellowship as we walked with the throng at the house of God." (Psalm 55:12-14) There was no place to hide: that friend/enemy knew where he lived.

The psalmist began by asking God to hear his prayer. We do not know whether he took action against his enemies, as we want to do and actually do—by gossiping, talking about our enemies to other people as a way to undercut their power over us—an approach that can so easily backfire and does not provide security or even relief. That is why there is something compelling about the poet's willingness to cry out to God. He turns his passion toward God instead of toward his own defence. David was not merely concerned for himself: "Confuse the wicked, O Lord, confound their speech, for I see violence and strife in the city. Day and night they prowl about on its walls; malice and abuse are within it. Destructive forces are at work in the city; threats and lies never leave its streets." (Psalm 55:9-11) Perhaps he wanted to flee because he perceived the immense harm that lurked about him. As a passionate man, he was not indifferent to his environment. Like him, we may long to run away from seeing what is really going on. Many of us have eyes to see and ears to hear—we are not rebellious—but we are weary with seeing and hearing what goes on in the world. We worry over a broken world that we cannot fix. We don't understand why people hurt one another when there is absolutely nothing of eternal or even lasting value to be gained by doing so.

The psalmist shifts his focus from evil and says "cast your cares on the Lord and he will sustain you; he will never let the righteous fall." (Psalm 55:22) How long did it take the poet to shift his gaze from destruction in the city to his love for God? How long does it take you to make that move? Have you made it? It is not easy and not automatic. It is an act of the will. Will you turn your attention to what you can do, what you can understand, regardless of how small your action seems and no matter how little you comprehend? The psalmist said "as for me, I trust in you." (Psalm 55:23b)

Lord, my trust is weak. Awaken me; sustain me through your name.

Creator God, help me to love the world, for your sake and to see

what is beautiful and hopeful in it.

Who's Afraid of Them?

When I am afraid I will trust in you.

In God, whose word I praise,

in God I trust; I will not be afraid.

What can mortals do to me?

Psalm 56:3-4

When opposition is carried to its ugliest extremes, when it becomes unremitting abuse, we are persuaded there is no place to hide from its power to track us down and punish us, just for being alive. The feeling that we cannot escape from someone's influence over us is terrifying, creating another feeling as well—that we have no value. If we feel these two emotions, they produce an absolute lack of safety, an abusive situation that robs us of the courage to resist power that seeks to overwhelm us. Children who have an abusive parent are locked in this fear. Adults that work in abusive environments are caught in this trap. These are feelings David conveyed: "Be merciful to me, O God, for enemies hotly pursue me; all day long they press their attack. My slanderers pursue me all day long; many are attacking me in their pride." (Psalm 56:1-2) We may have many enemies, or only one. It only takes one—a strong enemy can draw others to himself or herself; the others will help in the pursuit, even if it isn't their game. The power of opposition, in its extreme, convinces us that one person has all the power and that we have none. Without the power to resist—we have no voice and no value. At least, that is what the power to abuse wants us to believe, needs us to believe, for it to dominate. If we stop believing that we are worthless, the power of another person is seriously limited. The psalmist was specific about danger he felt: "all day long they twist my words; they are always plotting to harm me. They conspire, they lurk, they watch my steps, eager to take my life." (Psalm 56:5-6) The poet did not minimize his fear and the potential as well as real harm he suffered due to his enemies. He cried out to God to "record my lament; list my tears on your scroll—are they not in your record." (Psalm 56:8)

This was an amazing moment. While he was still afraid that he had no value and could be wiped out at any moment, he cried to God who both hears and sees his need. It is not simply that God saw and heard him. God paid so much attention, David imagined God writing down all his woes on a list that will be kept, that will not be forgotten. During this moment, the psalmist refused to continue feeling worthless. He said, "By this I will know that God is for me. In God, whose word I praise, in the Lord, whose word I praise—in God I trust; I will not be afraid. What can human beings do to me?" (Psalm 56:9b-11) Notice the repetition. The poet was utterly afraid but spoke to God as a way to gain courage, to lift his head, stand up straight. He chose to believe that God loved him and cared for his life; he was right. God loved him.

While going through a difficult time, a friend listened to me for a long while; then she said very kindly: "Stand up straight and lift your head." If we are beaten down by opposition that takes no account of our humanity, we wear that abuse bodily. We stoop, as if expecting to receive one more blow. It is remarkable what happens if we refuse to believe we have no value and reclaim our right to let God be the lifter of our heads. I do not say that simply believing we have value because we are God's beloved will end all the hostility we face. But we will be different. It is a beginning. Our enemy will notice.

Jesus, keep my feet from stumbling. Be the lifter of my head.

Keep my eyes on the horizon where you are, God. My help comes

from you. I know that you are my helper but I am afraid.

Let me see you standing with me, Jesus. Please help me so I can

focus my attention on what I want and what I need to do next.

Give me confidence to stand up straight because I know you are

the lifter of my head and you protect me, my Saviour and Friend.

Turn my attention to what can be done, instead of this focusing

on what I am afraid of—thank you.

I See Only Danger

I am in the midst of lions;
I lie among ravenous beasts—people
whose teeth are spears and arrows,
whose tongues are sharp swords.

Psalm 57:4

In the Old Testament enemies were other people. At least, that is an impression one gets from reading the psalms of opposition. It is an accurate reading of opposition and the fear that goes with it when others neither understand nor support us in important ways. Yet Jesus introduced an idea that alters our perception of enemies: he suggested we only have one enemy; the enemy of the soul is Satan. The army the Evil One deploys to our harm is the only real threat to our well-being if we follow Jesus. And he promised that he already won the battle against that enemy through his death on the cross and his resurrection to new life, which we share in because of him. (John 16:33) Yet we are well-advised to listen to the psalmist explain what it is like to be among those who do not love us and wish us ill—whether they are spiritual or human enemies.

In our psychological era, we tend to identify a struggle with Satan in our inner lives as an internal contest between an ego and its detractors—the voice of those who seem not to love or cherish us— who seem not to look out for our interests, but only seek after their own. Enemies may be parents, friends, colleagues, neighbors or acquaintances but have this in common—they do not meet our most basic needs for attention and respect. We are not well in their presence. If we do not get what we need, the loss is great. We cannot pretend loss is insignificant. We wear the evidence in our very being. It doesn't help to minimize suffering or talk ourselves out of being needy. We began life as infants, dependent on others. There is nothing wrong with our need for others. It is what it means to be human. How can we silence inner voices that enemies leave behind in our thought life? Can we garden our hearts in the same way we weed the soil and tend flowers in our backyards. If human loss is deep, its roots are also deep.

These roots go so deep, along with the psalmist, we cry for help and say that foes have spread their nets within our very soul. Harsh and accusing words echo in our minds. We cannot escape them, even when we are alone. In this psalm, we crouch by a solid rock with the poet as he cried out to the Lord for protection and took refuge in the shadow of his wings until disaster passed. The psalmist believed disaster would pass—he saw an end was possible—something that is hard to believe if we cannot see it yet. The poet was clear: he was unable to end his suffering in his own strength. He awaited rescue. Out of utter helplessness, he cried to God, acknowledging that he was hiding with no way to protect himself. He was at the end of his own resources; fear was his only companion. He held to one hope. God would hear him. He could not save himself but was steadfast. What does it mean to be steadfast when you are crouching beside a rock at the end of your own resources? It may be as simple as attending to intricate colors in the rock you hide behind or the pattern of the leaf of a tree. Let your eyes rest on their beauty so you are drawn, even for a moment, away from raucous voices within your heart, voices that move you to fear. If the only enemy is Satan, the only help is God. To silence Satan's voice, we call on the blood of Christ's sacrifice. We keep out of the way while God does battle.

Lord Jesus I'm helpless. I can't rescue myself. I abhor my weakness. I'm embarrassed but here it is; I cannot rescue myself. Let weakness open my heart to yours. I can see that loving me is your work, not mine. I am waiting. I ask for your help so I can breathe freely while I wait for you. Show me something beautiful as I ponder my situation and wait by the solid rock, Lord Jesus Christ. Now I know there is no beauty more amazing than your grace. Turn to me, Lord. Let me see you in a new way. Thank you.

Snarling Dogs

Powerful people conspire against me for no
offence or sin of mine, O Lord, I have done
no wrong, yet they are ready to attack me.

Psalm 59:3b-4a

Sometimes David was innocent. In this psalm he suffered but not because of his own sin. He was caught in a trap set by Saul, who had absolute power over him. In modern life, it is hard to feel innocent if we suffer the effects of abuse. It was like that during the French Revolution, which may seem unconnected to your life. Kings of France were consumed by ease; forcing people to conform to their whims, they allowed themselves to abuse those they were supposed to serve. Power can be like that: people are fascinated by the ease of getting what they want just because they can and no longer treat others as human—but mere objects they manipulate to get their way. Instead of resisting abuse, those abused may hide in their suffering, anger and humiliation. The French peasants revolted. David resisted by speaking of his innocence. If we silence our dream for authentic participation in a system that is overwhelming because of what some people do to us, we act as if we deserve what is happening—a complicit form of guilt David refused to own.

Leadership was never meant to become abuse. Scripture is clear. In 1 Samuel 8, the people asked for a king and Samuel was appalled. God was their king. Yet when they asked for a human king, God gave them one, with a warning. A human king would oppress them but they did not heed the warning. In giving them a king, God made a distinction between rulers and people to imply he expects us to remain obedient to him even if our kings do not: "Now here is the king you have chosen....If you fear the Lord and serve and obey him and do not rebel against his commands, and if both you and the king who reigns over you follow the Lord your God—good! But if you do not obey the Lord, and if you rebel against his commands, his hand will be against you." (1 Samuel 12:13-15) God warned that when power becomes domination, resisting that power appears so costly that we may fail to obey God, for example, by not using the gifts he gave us. We are caught in a trap, just as the leader is trapped inside the seductive sin of abusing others.

The psalm describes enemy abuse by pointing out "they return at evening, snarling like dogs, and prowl around the city. See what they spew from their mouths—they spew out swords from their lips, and they say, 'Who can hear us?' (Psalm (59:6-7) Abusive people believe everyone else is stupid, worthless, thinking that even God does not hear and cannot prevent them getting what they want. The psalmist knew that God sees and will consume them in wrath "till they are no more." (Psalm 59:13) The penalty for disobeying God by misusing power and failing to value others is annihilation. Punishment is built into the sin itself: abusers alienate themselves from human emotions and humane action. In a relentless pursuit to get what they want— they render themselves inhuman and cast themselves outside the kingdom of God. If those who suffer their abuse perceive its pattern, they open their eyes in sorrow and commit themselves to resisting the evil they see, with God's help.

Lord, I am scared. I am in what feels like an impossible situation. Please release me from feeling worthless and afraid. Let me know that you love me and my life is held in your hands. Give me wisdom to know how to remain true to you. This is your world. When you created it, you said it was good. Help me be part of that goodness—not because I am better or good in myself but because I am beloved by you. Help me find courage and opportunity to convey that you are a God of love. I know nothing can separate me from you: not danger, not other people, not my sense of being weak and afraid, not even this current situation. Let me love the world in your name. Help me feel the wind of your Spirit in the sails of my soul, Lord Jesus.

Holding Together

How long will you assault me? Would all
of you throw me down—this leaning wall,
this tottering fence? They fully intend to
topple me from my lofty place; they take
delight in lies. With their mouths they bless,
but in their hearts they curse.

Psalm 62:3-4

David learned to live in two worlds at the same time—one with God, one with enemies. When opposition became an all-out attack, he felt weak. He called himself a leaning wall, a tottering fence and acknowledged the strain suffered due to his enemies. But there was calm within the storm: "My soul finds rest in God alone; my salvation comes from him...Find rest, O my soul, in God alone; my hope comes from him." (Psalm 62:1, 5) Calm is not effortless; it's a balancing act between knowing God is our refuge and trying to practice that reality. David worked at being at peace—effort was expended to keep from falling apart yet he knew God's hand held him up. In his willingness to remain in a place of needing help and waiting on God, he found new insight to help him understand the human condition. If we are willing, suffering can teach us what it means to be human. These lessons cannot be got in any other way.

In his discomfort he perceived that "The lowborn are but a breath, the highborn are but a lie; if weighed on a balance they are nothing; together they are only a breath. Do not trust in extortion or take pride in stolen goods; though your riches increase, do not set your heart on them." (Psalm 62:9-10) In a tension of living in two worlds at once, he realized the significance of his life and grasped what really mattered—God alone was his fortress, he would not be shaken. What does it mean to find comfort in God alone? What is that comfort like? Is he saying that if trouble comes we should distance ourselves from other people and become a fortress? Is it wrong to tell other people our troubles and confide in them? Was he advocating that we should wall ourselves off from others? He said, "O people; pour out your heart to him, for God is our refuge." (Psalm 62:8) If we are oppressed, isn't being alone and lonely the biggest problem we face, along with feeling misunderstood? How could the poet find rest in God alone when his suffering had to do with people who populate the worlds he struggled between? How did he live in two worlds at the same time? As we read the psalm, we might hear echoes of Ecclesiastes with its whispers of despair. But David did not despair. He set his heart on God and learned to hear one thing that God had spoken, two things God's character conveyed: he knew "that you, O God, are strong, and that you, O Lord, are loving" (Psalm 62:11) a unity of insight fundamental to faith in God.

The psalmist came to see through suffering that two things are true about God. God is powerful. God is love. When this dyad breaks apart and people come to think that God is either powerful or loving but not both (in theological terms, the theodicy problem), faith breaks down. The psalmist perceives and accepts that these two ideas create one truth about God that cannot be severed. It is a remarkable vision, a unique insight about the God of Israel, which distinguishes God from all other gods. It is the heart of tension in suffering. How can I believe God is powerful and loving, given my situation? Either God loves me and would fix it but isn't strong enough, or else, God is strong but doesn't love me enough to rescue me from trouble.

Keeping these two ideas together and believing they are both true is a summons to trust. The psalmist heard the requirement and was trying; trust takes effort and does not eradicate anxiety.

Lord God, I do not know why I am still waiting for you to come

to help me, but I know you will come and will help. I feel skeptical

about other people right now; please relieve me of my mistrust.

Teach me how to wait. Help me hold together these two truths:

that you are loving; that you are good. Let me see you clearly.

The Uproar of Evil

Hear me, O God, as I voice my complaint;
protect my life from the threat of the enemy.
Hide me from the conspiracy of the wicked,
from that noisy crowd of evildoers.

Psalm 64:1-2

In general, the first line of every psalm reveals the passion on the poet's heart. If it is a psalm of praise, its first line will let us know it. The primary emotion for the oppressed is fear and this is a feeling the first line of Psalm 64 shouts out loud. If we are oppressed, dread infuses our waking thoughts and seeps into our midnight wakefulness. There is a great difference between fear and paranoia—fear is grounded on what is really happening; in paranoia, we lose touch with reality. The world around us needs to perceive the difference in what we say about our experience, but often does not. I spoke with a woman who shared the sense of oppression the psalmist depicted. At one point in our conversation, she seemed exasperated, saying, "I know I seem always to be talking about my troubles. I can't stop. But I haven't always been like this—I am not always like this. Why can't people hear that it is my pain talking? Why can't they see my suffering? Why can't they separate the real me from my problems? Why don't they see me at all?"

If someone is injured physically, we go to a hospital to visit them. If they are pale and crabby, if they eat Jell-O, not solid food, we understand what is going on and are patient. We leave them on the ward and go home while professionals administer their care. If someone is suffering because of unbearable loss, whether due to personal, institutional, or familial abuse, we might confuse the effects of harm for their essential personality and believe it is something about them that cannot change. This mistake is telegraphed to those who suffer and intensifies their pain. People that suffer ongoingly can make the same mistake; forgetting that there is more to them than what is currently going on, they can come to believe it is impossible to change. It is embarrassing to be in a state of suffering, as the woman I mentioned pointed out. Most of us are poor at perceiving the pattern of suffering that is due to oppression. We may not hear the justice in their cause if we have not experienced injustice as they have. We may not see how differences in terms of wealth, age, class, intelligence, race or culture create the conditions that are de-humanizing for them.

But God is just and sees evil. When losses are significant, we are caught in fear the poet recorded in the psalm. Fear relaxes as we realize that those who do evil are wrong to think God can neither hear nor see what they do. Psalm 94 declares, "take heed, you senseless ones among the people; you fools, when will you become wise? Does he who implanted the ear not hear? Does he who formed the eye not see? (Psalm 94:8-9) God will come and set things right. But can we wait for God's arrival? How are we to act as we wait? Those who suffer have a deep need to be believed. We enjoy relief if friends that are wise to suffering patiently hear our lament. As suffering adults, scripture invites us not to ignore injustice or remain trapped, but "if it is possible, as far as it depends on you, live at peace with everyone. Do not take revenge, my friends, but leave room for God's wrath, for it is written: It is mine to avenge; I will repay, says the Lord. On the contrary: 'If your enemies are hungry, feed them; if they are thirsty, give them something to drink. In doing this, you will heap burning coals on their heads'. Do not be overcome by evil, but overcome evil with good." (Romans 12:18-21) It is hard to step outside our suffering and return good for evil.

Lord Jesus, I don't know how to overcome evil with good.

I am not good enough to do it without your help. Pour your

holiness into my heart so I will not sin against you. Show me simple,

practical, active ways to bring health into my situation.

Help me carry them out wisely, without fear, for it is you that I serve.

You are my Lord and Saviour, in you I trust.

I'm Going Under

Save me, O God, for the waters have
come up to my neck. I sink in miry depths,
where there is no foothold. I have come
into the deep waters; the floods engulf me.
I am worn out calling for help; my throat is
parched. My eyes fail, looking for my God.
Those who hate me without reason
outnumber the hairs of my head; many
are my enemies without cause, those
who seek to destroy me. I am forced to
restore what I did not steal.

Psalm 69:1-4

Suffering is like drowning. In some psalms of opposition the poet declared his innocence; in others he confessed his guilt. In this psalm his situation is complex. He acknowledged sin: "You know my folly, O God; my guilt is not hidden from you." (Psalm 69:5) But he also said he lost his footing in a flood of consequences that arose with his wrongdoing that now overwhelm him; it was out of proportion to what he did: "I am forced to restore what I did not steal." (Psalm 69:4) Sometimes when we sin we get lucky: outcomes are small. Other times, the ripples from our sin continue relentlessly. We are stuck in consequences we cannot escape. Some people are pleased to intensify our pain and distress. Our suffering offers them a relief from dwelling on their own condition. Like children, they turn their backs to our shame, either because they see no way to help or else they think we are getting what we deserve. They harden their hearts to our weeping. The poet raged against them: "Pour out your wrath on them [God]; let your fierce anger overtake them. May their place be deserted; let there be no-one to dwell in their tents. For they persecute those you wound and talk about the pain of those you hurt." (Psalm 69:24-26) The poet heard his enemies whisper in the streets as he walked by. He felt their eyes on the back of his neck as he shuffled along the path.

However, he did not complain against God. He knew he suffered because of his own action. God had brought about the punishment his folly called for; yet he could not endure reactions from those that seemed unable to recognize themselves in his suffering and had no empathy for his sad state. Even his repentance sparked their scorn. The psalmist did not complain about his penalty since it was an expression of God's justice. He lamented the absence of empathy in those around who would not associate his suffering with times in their own lives when they suffered due to the results of their own sin. In an upsurge of spiritual pride, empathy dies. We worry about our own skin and cannot reach out to a sinner that wants to make amends. Our hearts harden.

In this psalm, we hear echoes of treatment Jesus suffered, though unlike the psalmist, he was entirely innocent of sin: "You know (God) how I am scorned, disgraced and shamed; all my enemies are before you. Scorn has broken my heart and has left me helpless; I looked for sympathy, but there was none, for comforters, but I found none. They put gall in my food and gave me vinegar for my thirst." (Psalm 69:19-21; Matthew 27:45-48) Unlike Jesus, David heard their scorn and called down the wrath of God on their heads. Jesus felt the scorn of his abusers and called out to God to forgive them since they did not know what they were doing. (Luke 23:34) We want to be like Jesus not David. But we are mistaken if we try to be like Jesus by minimizing suffering, pretending it's nothing really and doesn't affect us much. Jesus suffered mockery and did not pretend his pain was a trifle. He did not lie. He cried out to God. We can as well.

Lord, help me tell myself the truth. I am suffering because of my sin; I am not like you. But I want to be like you. Please rescue me from drowning. I cannot endure my pain. It is too much. Please help me. Lift my head. Loose my feet from the mud. I look for you. I wait for you. I will turn my gaze away from those who cannot find empathy for me in their hearts. Lord Jesus, come.

Have Mercy

Yet I am poor and needy;
come quickly to me, O God.
You are my help and my deliverer;
O Lord, do not delay.

Psalm 70:5

This psalm is an S.O.S.—an expression of urgent need: Save our souls. In sending an S.O.S. those in danger have no time to spell it out. Help is needed urgently. There is no time for reasoned argument, no time for persuasion. Rescue is essential. Everything depends on whether someone hears the cry for help. If no one is listening, sailors drown in a wild sea; miners are buried in lightless, dense earth; pilot and crew go down in a burning plane, lost in Arctic snow. One of the strangest aspects of crying for help is the timing between a last, effective cry, when God actually arrives to rescue, and cries for help prior to that successful one, when no help seems to come—yet. How much trouble do we need to be in before God will come to our aid? Is there a magic moment? "Now it is really bad, Lord. I think I can endure no longer. Come now, please." Does God wait for the perfect time? What would make the moment perfect? Do we have to be in a right state of acceptance and humility before God in order to prepare for rescue? Is being rescued about getting into an acceptable frame of mind to prepare for it—something like waiting in line outside in the cold to pay for our ticket before we get to enjoy the show?

Suffering tests belief. The psalmist was caught in a trap he wanted to escape but he made two requests that tell the truth: "May those who seek my life be put to shame and confusion...May all who seek you (God) rejoice and be glad in you." (Psalm 70:2; 4) He offered fundamental insight. We cannot control God through a call for help. We are at God's mercy. God sees the whole of experience and perceives the big picture. God will come when God will come. We wait for him to speak to our hearts; God speaks when God speaks. Have we no influence or control over the timing? Are we helpless before God? Yes we are. Yet, when God comes, waiting makes sense. How do you feel about your helplessness while you wait? What will you do during that helpless state? Where will you put your faith? What will you count on as you wait for God and cry out for help? The greatest test in trouble has to do with humility. Will we be so angry at our helplessness and the humiliation we feel because of it that we turn away from God and refuse to wait for him any longer? How can we understand being in relationship with God if nothing we do influences his arrival? Surely, in a relationship, both parties affect what happens. What are we supposed to be doing while we wait? How do we keep waiting and also keeping believing God will come?

These questions are difficult because they assume that God is not present and suddenly is present when he rescues us. But we know that God is always, everywhere present. How could God seem not to be there? How do we make sense of these questions; they are part of suffering itself? This aspect of suffering is epistemological. It can drive us to distraction. We feel an intellectual pain when we are unable to make sense of what is going on. We cannot understand what God is doing because his apparent absence is out of sync with past experience. God has rescued us before and spoken to us in the past. Why is he not doing so now? The psalmist simply put it all on the table before

God—whom he did not doubt would rescue him. But he strained to believe; he worked to stay in that place of resting and not turning away.

Lord, please come to help me. I have no idea why you have

not yet come. From my perspective, it is way past the perfect time.

I don't know what you want me to do. I simply put my need

before you, like David, and I commit to trusting you. You have come

to help me in the past. You don't change. I will wait.

Come quickly, Lord.

Can Anyone Hear Me?

Do not cast me away when I am old;
do not forsake me when my strength is
gone. For my enemies speak against me;
those who wait to kill me conspire together.
They say, 'God has forsaken him; pursue
him and seize him, for no-one will rescue
him. Be not far from me, O God; come
quickly, O my God, to help me.

Psalm 71:9-12

If we take the psalms of opposition together, it seems as if the poet is always upset. His situation reminds me of a painted scene of orderly modern adults in a park. They are all dressed perfectly; parasols held with composure, in the right place at the right time, calm, rational, deliberate, under control. No one is looking at a child in the middle of the painting who is crying out loud. Once you see the child, you no longer see beauty in the adults but only indifference and neglect.

How often we feel like a child in Seurat's painting.[11] We cry aloud as silently as the child in the picture. I believe the poetry of writing psalms was like that for David. He cried out loud, unheard by those around him. There is one way in which the psalmist is not like the child in the painting. David knew that God was viewing the picture. God sees the child; God sees the neglect. He was confident: "Since my youth, O God, you have taught me...to this day I declare your marvelous deeds. Even when I am old and grey, do not forsake me, O God, until I declare your power to the next generation, your might to all who are to come." (Psalm 71:17-18) The whole point of loss and recovery, the reason for learning to lose important things and regain our sense of balance afterwards, the whole point of our lives is to be examples to those that come after us. We show the way; we do not neglect the young. We are responsible for living in a manner that encourages the young to grow up and live well. To be that example, we must learn our lessons well.

If adults do not grow up, why should children? The poet said, "Who, O God, is like you? Though you have made me see troubles, many and bitter, you will restore my life again; from the depths of the earth you will once again bring me up. You will increase my honour and comfort me once again." (Psalm 71:19b-21) David needed comfort that, as viewers, we wish we could offer the isolated child in Georges Seurat's painting, one lost in a forest of unmoved, pre-occupied adults. As viewers, we cannot be indifferent to those adults. They are doing something wrong—neglect is evil; it is a sin that many children suffer until they come to think God cares nothing for them.

We are not unmoved by the evil some people do, even though we live in a culture that believes it is proper to be nice to everyone, regardless of their actions. The psalms are not concerned to say nice things about people who are evil. Being silent about evil does not help us be compassionate towards those who do wrong in God's sight. Jesus summons us to love our enemies, not overlook them. The psalmist's expression of confidence that God saw his life and knew what was going on led him to offer praise, "I will praise you with the harp for your faithfulness, O my God; I will sing praise to you with the lyre, O Holy One of Israel. My lips will shout to you—I, whom you have redeemed. My tongue will tell of your righteous acts all day long...those who wanted to harm me have been put to shame and confusion." (Psalm 71:22-24)

Lord, please help me sort out how I feel towards those who have harmed me and still do. Let me sense deeply in my heart that you see my life and do not turn away from me when I cry out to you. You hear me. Thank you, Lord God Almighty, lover of my soul. You keep me in the palm of your hand. My life is not hidden from you. You know it completely, Lord. From the time I was born you see me. Help me understand that being seen by you is my greatest good—and the satisfaction of my deepest need.

Utterly Destroy!

O God, whom I praise, do not be silent, for people
who are wicked and deceitful have opened their
mouths against me...With words of hatred they
surround me; they attack me without cause. In
return for friendship they accuse me, but I turn
to prayer....Appoint someone evil to oppose [my
enemy]; let an accuser stand at his right hand.
When he is tried, let him be found guilty, and may
his prayers condemn him. May his days be few;
may another take his place of leadership.
May his children be fatherless and his wife a widow.
May his children be wandering beggars; may they
be driven from their ruined homes. May a creditor
seize all he has; may strangers plunder the fruits
of his labor. May no-one extend kindness to him
or take pity on his fatherless children. May his
descendents be cut off, their names blotted oul
from the next generation. May the iniquity of his
fathers be remembered before the Lord; may the
sin of his mother never be blotted out. May their
sins always remain before the Lord, that he may
cut off the memory of them from the earth.

Psalm 109:1-15

In this psalm, the poet moved from despair to rage. He spewed out
ways an enemy could be cut off from the community. His wanted to

ex-communicate someone he hated. In the twenty-first century, it is hard to realize the extent of harm he wished on someone he felt had caused so much pain. If we are angry, it helps to realize how far the poet went in expressing his anger to God. He raged against someone who "never thought of doing a kindness," hounded the poor, the needy and the brokenhearted; someone who "wore cursing like a garment" and "found no pleasure in blessing" other people. (Psalm 109:16-18) His enemy hurt many more people in addition to the poet and was someone who caused harm to those that were already weak and oppressed. David felt angry at injustice. And so he should. Yet in his anger, he turned to prayer. What does turning to prayer say about David's understanding of his relationship to God?

Perhaps he prayed to keep himself from retaliation. That is an excellent use of prayer. Take it to the Lord and leave it there. Instead of fighting back directly, rather than becoming what he hated in his enemy, he invoked God's wrath upon an injustice he was certain God would judge in the same way he did. He knew what drew out the wrath of God and was justified in his complaint. In anguish due to his suffering, because he was weary with having to watch other people suffer, he was fading away like a shadow. His suffering, his judgment of the wrong evil people were committing, produced sorrow in which he saw himself as disgusting in other people's sight. He felt "shaken off like a locust," (Psalm 109:23) an object of scorn to those who could not see in him the results of a human pattern of oppression. He was angry at all injustice!

He called to God, asking to be saved—another good use of prayer. Confident God would bless him, he was beset by people who did not perceive what his enemy was able to accomplish; others began to curse him. (Psalm 109:28-29) His enemy had persuasive power to get others to see the poet only as an object—something to abuse. Enemies often manage to alter onlooker perceptions so that we are helpless to defend ourselves against those who casually turn away and we are "clothed with disgrace and wrapped in shame as in a cloak." (Psalm 109:29) The poet captured the feeling precisely: trapped by harm, he was abused with passerby judgments hardened into a belief that his abuse was well deserved. Onlooker reactions are echoed in those who find street people disgusting because they smell, without considering that they have no place to get washed because they live on the street. The poet's anger was for himself and for others:

Jesus, here is my anger. Rescue me! I am afraid to keep

holding on to it. I am afraid to let it go. I need your help.

Waiting for a Sign

Teach me your way, O Lord, and I will walk
in your truth; give me an undivided heart,
that I may fear your name. I will praise you,
O Lord, my God, with all my heart; I will
glorify your name for ever....Give me a sign
of your goodness, that my enemies may see
it and be put to shame, for you, O Lord,
have helped me and comforted me.

Psalm 86:11-12, 17

The psalmist talked to himself. We note several examples of conver-sations he had with his own soul. "Why are you downcast, O my soul? Why so disturbed within me? Put your hope in God, for I will yet praise him, my Savior and my God." (Psalm 42:11) And "Why are you down-cast, O my soul? Why so disturbed within me? (Psalm 43:5) "Praise the Lord, O my soul; all my inmost being, praise his holy name. Praise the Lord, O my soul, and forget not all his benefits—who forgives all your sins and heals all your diseases, who redeems your life from the pit and crowns you with love and compassion, who satisfies your desires with good things so that your youth is renewed like the eagle's." (Psalm 103:1-5) The struggle of learning through loss to recovery is a spiritual conversation we have in our own souls. Disturbances in the soul leave us with a divided heart. We are caught in a storm that does not offer safe harbor or calm assurance that God loves us. So we must talk to ourselves. Jesus understood our divided hearts. He said, "Out of the overflow of the heart the mouth speaks." (Matthew 12:34b) We speak to our souls, as David did, if we want to be well. What sign does your heart long for as evidence that God loves you?

David wanted a sign he could show others. We need people to recognize we are God's beloved, that we are not abandoned by God. But we may be harder on ourselves than the poet's enemies were on him. We cower before an inner rebuke, an accusing finger, a hand holding a sharp stick to pierce our confidence and deflate the hope we carry in our hearts. Recovery involves the imagination; it is ours and God's work. It is up to us to praise God. It is up to us to recall what God has done in the past that worked for our good. It is up to us to let God forgive us and heal our diseases, redeem our lives from the pit, crown us with love and compassion. It is up to us to put our faith in a God who promises to satisfy our desires with good things so we can be renewed with eagle's strength. It is hard to praise God and remember his benefits while immersed in sorrow, hard to enjoy God's promises if we allow suffering to persuade us that we are worthless. The soul's work is to recognize and resist effects of suffering that interfere with a capacity to receive what is good from God. Being active in praise strikes at the cynicism stored up in the soul; actively receiving God's presence is a way forward from loss to recovery. Both of these activities depend for their effectiveness on feeling connected to God.

Human spirituality is "a sense of felt connection."[12] All our experience, from birth onwards, is stored in the soul, in imagination and memory; it acts back on us to convey what the world is really like, what we are really like, and what we can expect in the future. Imagination is central to loss and recovery. Human reason may tell us what is true, but imagination tells us what is real.[13] The soul (a place spirituality stores its memories) is like a warehouse of images, feelings and beliefs. The soul must be persuaded to let its wares be sorted and re-organized if we want to recover from losses. Our identity has been shaped by memories, so we are not quite sure what we might gain and lose if we get well.

Lord Jesus, you know what is stored in my heart.

Receive my feeble praise. Unclutter me. Burn my cynicism.

I am full of worry, sin, sadness, bad experience, disappointment.

Can you renew someone like me?

Lord Jesus Christ, help me with my unbelief.

Trouble on Every Side

Rescue me, O Lord, from evildoers;
protect me from the violent, who devise
evil plans in their hearts and stir up war
every day. They make their tongues as
sharp as a serpent's; the poison of vipers
is on their lips....The proud have hidden
a snare for me; they have spread out the
cords of their net and have set traps for
me along the path.

Psalm 140:1-3, 5

A theme of what might sound like paranoia runs through psalms of opposition. How can we recognize suffering when we listen to someone? Consider this story. Judy is in her forties and has no children. Her husband makes a good salary so she decided to leave her teaching position to work for a Mission Agency. While teaching, she was Vice-Principal of her large urban high school where she had a lot of responsibility. She joined the Agency nine years ago to coordinate relationships between churches and missionaries, linking local communities with churches around the world. Her program was under a general Director; she had no decision-making power. Recently, the Director offered her a new job in Funding and Recruitment, one that came with more money and greater responsibility. She weighed a number of issues and prayerfully considered the opportunity but sensed no inclination to change. She felt called to her program; a sense of call that had not diminished. She turned down the offer.

As a result of her reflection, she decided to approach the Director for a raise. In her nine years with the Agency, she had no increase in salary. Four times the number of people now worked in her program than when she started. It was successful in the best sense. She thought that if the Director offered a higher salary for the position she rejected, there might be more money. Others people had just got a raise. She gathered documentation to support her request and asked to see him. At the meeting she presented her case. When she handed him her documents, he threw them on the floor, scattering them everywhere. He raised his arms and yelled something. She heard the word greed but couldn't hear the rest of the sentence clearly. He hollered: "You were deceitful and sneaky to collect information behind my back?" She was stunned and got up from her chair and left the office. She managed to keep from crying until she was back at her desk and closed the door. She sat in her chair, wondering what to do next, while she tried to regain composure.

You may have a complex response to Judy's story. You may want more information. Yet we can see she has an enemy like the psalms speak about. She is afraid of someone with power to make work unbearable. She can see the Director's behaviour as unacceptable, even if he had reasons to reject her request. He cancelled the possibility of dialogue in advance by yelling and throwing down her papers. None of us can justify before God setting up unjust boundaries. Judy may agree with the psalmist that such people should be surrounded by trouble; burning coals should come down on their heads; they should fall in miry pits, never to rise. (Psalm 140:9-10) But she may also feel afraid, worthless and hopeless. We often blame ourselves instead of holding others accountable when they are unjust. Unlike the poet, we might assume we deserve bad treatment. Perhaps, like the Director, you have come to believe you have a right to express whatever you happen to feel. Lowliness and haughtiness are misguided. They support oppression.

Lord Jesus, be the lifter of my head. Reveal to me what is happening in my relationships. Give me your view of injustice. Jesus, have mercy. Let me see when I am unjust. Let me hear my tone of voice when I speak to people but feel threatened and frustrated. Allow me to see my actions as you see them. Let me sense what it is like for others to be in my presence. Lord, have mercy on me. Show me how to love others. I want to participate in a loving community. Show me daily how to do that.

Nowhere to Hide

I cry aloud to the Lord;...I pour out my
complaint before him; before him I tell my
trouble. I have no refuge; no one cares for
my life. I cry to you, O Lord;...you are my
refuge....You are my portion in the land of
the living. Listen to my cry, for I am in
desperate need; rescue me from those who
pursue me, for they are too strong for me.
Set me free from my prison, that I may
praise your name.

Psalm 142:1-7

Perhaps you have, like me, heard a Holocaust survivor tell his story. Those who suffer abuse are compelled to tell their stories over and over again. As they relate the story, they actually relive it. As its familiar parts unfold, the speaker is caught between past and present. Finishing the story allows them to move through the memory emotionally so they come out on the other side, so to speak. While they are telling the story, there is a look of intensity on their faces, a rush of words that are telltale signs of the currency their narratives hold. I have seen that expression on faces of people who recount the Holocaust or else convey abandonment that happened when they were young. The pattern is clear. A storyteller is caught between past and present; both frames of reference are real—the past invades the present, disturbing the storyteller in ways similar to the abuse itself. If you are the listener, you might think it is harmful to retell stories of abuse. I think you are not right—whether they are your stories or tell of someone else's sorrow. Recall the Wailing Wall, a holy site, a place stories are told again and again. The stones do not tire of hearing a lament; they do not turn away. But people get weary with hearing stories of woe. It is a rare friend that will listen to a whole narrative without conveying they are frustrated or fatigued.

As I read Psalm 142, I have the feeling the poet had come to the end of people's patience for listening to his sorry situation. No one wanted to hear it again. No one saw the story itself as part of the abuse he suffered as well as part of its cure. In sorrow, he was locked inside a debate with himself. The story is like a puzzle he is trying to solve—it continues to evade solution but he was compelled to keep trying to work it out. The compulsion to repeat the tale, and the reality that it tires people out to keep hearing it, drew him into God's presence. That was a good place to end up. I honour the choice he made to let God be Listener. God is like a Cosmic Therapist, listening attentively, without turning away, yet God is not indifferent to how our stories end. God listens, as the psalmist said. He is the only friend we have that has no personality problems of his own. Everyone else has a limitation for listening to a sufferer's sad song.

Facing other people's fatigue with our suffering may be a stimulus to move on to try to get well. Being told to move on by someone who is not listening usually makes things worse. It would be a better world if more people were able to listen to a whole story so its owner could feel neither crazy nor alone. We want a witness. We need to see a facial reaction to horror or injustice that happened to us. We long for others who have gone through hard times to name what is going on. We feel profound relief when our experience is really heard—its burden lightens. It is one thing to suffer injustice and quite another to feel we are the only one who has gone through it because no one comes alongside to carry the burden and let us tell the story that has locked us inside it. This is the prison the psalmist experienced.

Heavenly Father, release me from feeling alone, strange, stranded
on an island of experience that makes no sense to anyone else.
I cannot bear isolation any longer. Crack open the door of my cell.
Let me see some daylight. Send someone who can listen to my story
and not turn away from my need to be heard. Help me Lord.
I am so tired of being trapped inside a sad story but I need some
help to open the door and get out of it.

The Golden Rule

Set a guard over my mouth, O Lord;

keep watch over the door of my lips.

Let not my heart be drawn to what is evil,

to take part in wicked deeds with those

who are evildoers; let me not eat of

their delicacies.

Psalm 141: 3

We must acknowledge that an unhindered use of power becomes a pleasure we do not want to give up. If this were not so, our world would be more just. There is something seductive about getting what we want and making other people obey our whims. As the poet said, unjust action has its reward—it is one of the delicacies the evil devour. Unhindered power is addictive. It is a tasty treat we can no longer refuse to consume. That is why the psalmist distinguished between those who commit sin, as he did himself, and those who are evil because they enjoy betraying other people. David prayed, "do not grant the wicked their desires, O Lord; do not let their plans succeed, or they will become proud." (Psalm 140:8) He spotted the trap of gaining asymmetrical power over others—he perceived the pattern and knew that life for the wicked is out of control.

A way out of the trap for those committed to evil is to experience their own abuse. As the poet said, "Let the heads of those who surround me be covered with the trouble their own lips have caused." (Psalm 140:9) Did he simply want to hurt evil people as they had hurt him? Was he focused on retribution, calling down God's wrath as a way to secure revenge? Maybe; he seemed to think wrongs he suffered, and witnessed happening to others, justified retribution. Yet there is a difference between wanting justice—longing for the wicked to finally see what they do that destroys the humanity of other people—and being consumed by revenge. The difference is a capacity for self-reflection. There is serious self-reflection in Psalm 141. The poet is willing to be corrected, "Let a righteous person strike me—that is a kindness; let them rebuke me—that is oil on my head. My head will not refuse it." (Psalm 140:5) (Righteous people do not strike someone to make a point.)

What he could not bear is correction from the wicked. We relate to his frustration. Consider those who claim, "I am saying this for your own good" and proceed to heap unwarranted, overwhelming, imbalanced criticism on us that crushes our humanity, though they profess the pure motive of wanting to help us see things as they really are. We feel in our bones they have no intention to rescue us from our suffering. Their words form a tighter trap?

I recall a conversation with a friend in which she confessed an addiction to gossip and pointed out what she realized about her habit that moved her to stop. Early on, she persuaded herself that gossip was a way to help other people. She passed on information because she told herself that third parties would offer more kindness if they heard the intimate details that she knew. One day someone circulated indelicate details about her and replied when challenged that "I thought it would help the situation if everyone understood why you act the way you do." My friend saw through her self-deception. She gossiped to make herself feel important. Telling stories about others gave her something to say. People listened when she held out juicy bits of data as the bait for their full attention. When the tables turned, she was appalled by herself. It was easier to stop gossiping than she imagined, once she realized before God what she had been doing.

Lord, you see what I am doing and you know why I do it.

Give me eyes to see and ears to hear myself so I honour you with

my words and deeds throughout this day. Help me love others the way

I want to be loved. Heal my hearing and restore my vision so that

I can perceive the truth about my actions and my intentions.

Apart from you, I cannot do what really matters in your Kingdom.

Please help me follow a rule you set out so long ago that I seldom

heed—it is as precious as gold and as rare.

To Forgive, to Forget

> He said to them, 'When you pray, say:
> Father, hallowed be your name,
> your kingdom come.
> Give us each day our daily bread.
> Forgive us our sins, for we also
> forgive everyone who sins against us.
> And lead us not into temptation.'
>
> **Luke 11:2-4**

Jesus taught his disciples to pray. In praying, he juxtaposed forgiving and being forgiven: forgive us our sins as we forgive others. Further, he said we should ask not to be led into temptation. The implications of the Lord's Prayer go very deep. I want to focus on a relationship that helps explain loss and recovery. Forgiveness is a process in which we resist temptation. When we are harmed we want to retaliate. A desire for revenge is a normal human reaction because, in being harmed, we lose face. Even if we forgive, we still have losses to deal with that are enduringly significant. These losses can drive us to seek revenge if we do not find a way to be relieved of them and to recover.

The word forgiveness has many words like it; for example: remit, pardon, appease, moderate, abate or slacken. These words suggest that someone who forgives sin relieves people of having to repay the full price of what they did. Some translations of the Lord's Prayer compare sin to being in debt or trespassing. Forgive our debts as we forgive others; forgive our trespasses as we forgive those who trespass against us. One metaphor is based on money owed, the other on land that is violated. Someone failed to repay a debt; someone dishonoured an established boundary. In both metaphors, due to sin, something is lost. These losses imply another one—the loss of trust in people who fail to pay what they owe or cut across boundaries we had a right to maintain. The Hebrew language has three words for forgiveness:[14] *kipper* (cover, pardon, forgiveness); *nasa* (lift up, carry away); *salach* (let go). All three imply removing sin but *kipper* and *salach* are used of God only. With *nasa*, sin ceases to cause a barrier between people. But with *kipper*, sin is covered so that it is no longer thrust between God and us. In the word *salach*, sin is forgiven so there is no resentment or anger in the mind of the injured party. God alone is able to forgive in the third sense of not holding a grudge. God does not lose face when someone sins. God does not become resentful.

People, in contrast, struggle with resentment—a deep sense that social honour and obligations due them (as child, parent, worker, participant or spouse) have not been granted—a pervasive human problem God does not have. In human interactions there is always resentment if we are wronged. An injured party is resentful and internally compelled to seek satisfaction. Forgiveness can satisfy the injured person if those who wronged them realize what they did: the injured party regains face. Repentant sinners make a sacrifice, an apology, to signify they are making amends and understand the harm they caused. But sacrifices do little good unless they are accompanied by sound ethical and humanitarian conduct—a change in the way we act. For a sacrifice to be effective there must be a change of heart. Forgiveness in scripture sometimes is conditioned by repentance which links us with renewed ethical conduct so that relationships are restored to enjoy their former blessings. With true repentance, there is no limit to forgiveness. God actively and personally forgives every repentant heart. But some who are injured get no satisfaction for their loss and cannot stop striving to try to recover face. Caught in a cycle of desire that perpetually evades them, they enjoy no rest. The cycle is entirely understandable. Are you someone who is caught in the desire to regain what you have lost? Is there someone you love who is trapped in this way? The problem is in seeing the difference between seeking reasonable satisfaction so you can regain face and seeking revenge.

Lord Jesus, help me sense the difference between my need to regain face and my longing to get revenge. Please don't stop instructing my heart. Don't abandon me, Lord. Please relieve my shame.

Let the Meditations of My Heart

Search me, O God, and know my heart;

test me and know my anxious thoughts.

See if there is any offensive way in me,

and lead me in the way everlasting."

Psalm 139:23-24

There is a pattern I see in my life that is a human tendency. It motivates action Freud named in his essay, the Omnipotence of Thought.[15] It goes something like this: I get an idea about others that I believe to be so true I don't question it. Then, I act toward others as if it is true. Take an attitude toward a colleague. Suppose he is essential to the institution where I work but I fear he will leave for somewhere better. As a result, I feel his rejection in advance, as if he was already gone. I feel anger and withdraw support in subtle ways. I treat him as an enemy and in so doing I harm our relationship. I have no direct evidence he wants to leave; it's a hunch. But it is enough to make me relate to him in a way that hurts us both—so subtly. That pattern of trusting hunches and not checking them out is one I must challenge and change if I want to be a follower of Jesus. Often these negative hunches are based on fear and the ways we have suffered in the past.

David took the problems he had with enemies to God. The moment we take troubles to the Lord, we release ourselves from the trap of private thinking. We let these thoughts be seen by God and we become accountable for them. It is hard to know if our thoughts about someone are correct. May the words of my mouth and the meditation of my heart be acceptable unto you, O Lord, my Rock and my Redeemer—is a theme that runs through the psalms. Jesus told us to attend to the plank in our own eye rather than fretting over the speck in someone else's. (Matthew 7:3-5) He did not say other people are free of wooden planks while we are not; he said taking care of our eyes is personal spiritual work. He shifted attention from paying back enemies to praying for them. I am not saying other people bear no responsibility for harm they cause. But, just as Judas did to Jesus, we hurt others if we turn away from them and turn them over to the Evil One. Judas was wrong about Jesus. We betray others if we put all our trust in our assumptions about what is going on with them and never ask questions. Turning away can be a small, insignificant act, a kiss, a wink—to incalculable cost for those our actions betray. I suggest that you, like me, turn away from people who need support because of hunches that we do not check out. Let us learn to turn people over to the Holy One rather than turning away from them, even if they cause us pain.

The psalmist turned his enemies over to God. He did not withhold expressions of anger, fear or a longing to recover from shame and be restored to his community. These passions drove the psalms of opposition. But there were ways he did not act if he lived up to his own insight. He didn't seek personal or public revenge. He continued to see God as just and loving. He continued to trust God to help him. When I say we are all guilty of abandoning support of other people and hence hand them over to the Evil One, I do not imply that we should just let other people hurt us. David wanted to be restored into community. If we let people harm us, we drown in shame and cannot enjoy healthy connection to those who are deceived by or inattentive to what is happening to us. I only say that taking revenge doesn't work very well. Instead, I invite you to acknowledge your enemies and take them to God.

Lord Jesus, help me believe you love me, though you know what I too have done to others. Let the knowledge of my own sin help me find a way to recover from the harm that I feel so deeply. Allow me to see how to love those who hurt me so the harm they cause is relieved and lessened. I want justice, Lord. Help me find a way to love people so I contribute to just action myself. Help me breathe freely in your presence so that I can hold my head up while I'm with others. Please Lord, I want to live life in your freedom, not in my fear.

Let Me See You

Hear my prayer, O Lord; let my cry for help
come to you. Do not hide your face from me
when I am in distress. Turn your ear to me;
when I call, answer me quickly. For my
days vanish like smoke; my bones burn like
glowing embers. My heart is blighted and
withered like grass; I forget to eat my food.
Because of my loud groaning I am reduced
to skin and bones. I am like a desert owl,
like an owl among the ruins. I lie awake;
I have become like a bird alone on a roof.
All day long my enemies taunt me; those
who rail against me use my name as a
curse. For I eat ashes as my food and
mingle my drink with tears because of your
great wrath, for you have taken me up and
thrown me aside. My days are like the
evening shadow; I wither away like grass.

Psalm 102:1-11

Suffering devastates the body. In this psalm, the poet was at the end
of his endurance. He cried out, certain that God is there. Where does
his confidence come from? He offered two clues. He believed God was
better than a human being. He spoke about Zion, and said, "For her
stones are dear to your servants; her very dust moves them to pity."
(Psalm 102:14) Then he reasoned that if ordinary people value stones

scattered over the ground, God in heaven cares for those he has created. As aspect of faithful belief is a choice to believe that God is better than humanity despite what is happening, even though God has not rescued us yet. In Western history, atheism results from believing the opposite: thinking that human beings are better, more compassionate, quicker to come to our aid than is the Almighty. While we suffer, we can be tempted to diminish God's greatness due to the losses we experience. David held firm to his trust in God.

A second insight came to the suffering poet: God will remain when all else now living passes away. His suffering would come to an end and God would still be God. His trust was unshaken; he was like Habakkuk who said, "though the fig-tree does not bud and there are no grapes on the vines, though the olive crop fails and the fields pro-duce no food, though there are no sheep in the pen and no cattle in the stalls, yet I will rejoice in the Lord, I will be joyful in God my Saviour." (Habakkuk 3:17-18) Habakkuk came to his commitment after searching out God, questioning the Lord. Do we expect to slip easily into trust, like people who slide their feet into warm slippers? It was not easy for Old Testament prophets to trust God. They cried in complaint and questioned God until they came to an understanding that surpassed human wisdom. It is only as we suffer deeply and recover from it that we see how humanity is purified through suffering. We can say with James, "Consider it pure joy, my brothers and sisters, whenever you face trials of many kinds, because you know that the testing of your faith develops perseverance. Perseverance must finish its work so that you may be mature and complete, not lacking any-thing." (James 1:2-4)

The psalmist believed that his own ability to love creation, even its dust, came from God. He clung to that assurance and called for help. Suffering can lead us in a different direction. It can drive us to disappointment with God that is so powerful we imagine that, if we were in God's place, we would not abandon human beings to the painful experience that dries up our bones and makes us eat ashes for food. Surely, this is a hard struggle—to trust God in the midst of feeling crushed by circumstances, or by intentional harm someone wrecked upon us when they betrayed our most basic human need for kindness and understanding. But it is also a good struggle.

Lord, my bones cry out to you. They are as dry as dust at my feet. But I know that you are here. I cling to the assurance that nothing has changed your love for me; nothing ever can. I know I will enjoy good days while I live on the earth. Lord, I believe. Help me with my unbelief. Come rescue me.

Let This Mind Be in You

Whatever happens, conduct yourselves in
a manner worthy of the gospel of Christ....
stand firm in one spirit, striving together
with one accord for the faith of the gospel
without being frightened in any way by
those who oppose you....For it has been
granted to you on behalf of Christ not only
to believe on him, but also to suffer for him,
since you are going through the same struggle
you saw I had, and now hear I still have.

Philippians 1:27-30

The good news is that suffering is part of the Christian life. The bad news is that sometimes we suffer for reasons not congruent with Christ's suffering and its purposes in the Kingdom of God. We are like Christ in that we suffer due to sin someone else initiated. We suffer because we live in a material world that sinful, harmful actions affect. Material effects have inertia (relentless motion) built into them that keep influencing us even if we receive forgiveness and forgive other people. Forgiveness does not erase harmful effects of sin. We forgive others to *start* a process of learning how to live with what they did to us, not as a way to eradicate harm they've done. But we are also unlike Christ in that we suffer because of sin we commit ourselves. Unlike him, we can be unaware of harmful effects of sin that remain unresolved in our very being. We suffer loss due to what people have done to us; we suffer loss due to what we have done to others. As a result, learning through loss and recovery is a primary task for Christians. Understanding loss and recovery is at the core of realizing the fullness of Christ in our lives as mature believers. We only address the significance of forgiveness if we acknowledge harm that sin causes: sin creates loss. Loss is a fundamental reality. Learning to be like Christ moves us through loss to recovery. Christianity responds to loss. Learning through loss and recovery is a partner with forgiveness. Together they release the benefits of being renewed in Christ Jesus.

In Christian community, we speak of forgiveness a great deal and we have many, varied feelings about these conversations. Yet we seldom take time, in my experience, to lament losses that sin wrecks upon us and our communities. Loss and recovery are expressed by the Incarnation. In Philippians, we read that communion with Christ is informed by his loss of equality with God as he came down to earth to save us from sin. Jesus, "being in very nature God, did not consider equality with God something to be grasped, but made himself nothing, taking the very nature of a servant, being made in human likeness....he humbled himself and became obedient to death—even death on a cross!" (Philippians 2:6-8) He took on our worst that we might enjoy God's best.

It is timely to take stock of our losses. It is healing to acknowledge the recovery Christ makes possible. The heart of recovery is found in resurrection. As we read about Christ, after his death, "God exalted him to the highest place and gave him the name above every name, that at the name of Jesus every knee should bow, in heaven and on earth and under the earth, and every tongue confess that Jesus Christ is Lord, to the glory of God the Father." (Philippians 2:9-11) Resurrection is a real and future hope. It is the model for life on earth as we turn losses over to Jesus, who suffered death and rose again and walks with us through the turmoil. We cannot learn from our losses if we minimize them. We do not escape them by drowning in them. What are we to do? We move through loss to recovery by paying attention to our sorrow. Giving heed to harm and hurt teaches us to know God, focuses attention on Christ's death and resurrection, lets us see that the future is in his hands and hopeful.

Lord Jesus, I have so many conflicting feelings. Let me see

that suffering is real and has a pattern you understand, even if

I don't. Let me know you love me. I need wisdom from above

and trust that you will give it generously, even to me.

Let Morning Come

Let the morning bring me word of your
unfailing love, for I have put my trust in you.
Show me the way I should go, for to you
I lift up my soul. Rescue me from my enemies, O Lord, for I hide myself in you.
Teach me to do your will, for you are my
God; may your good Spirit lead me on
level ground....in your righteousness,
bring me out of trouble.

Psalm 143:8-10, 11b

Every day is a new dawn; but if people are drowning in sorrow, this does not seem like the truth. How does it happen that we finally lift our heads from the pillow of our distress to look outside? What does it take for the daylight to lessen the burden and relieve sorrow? I don't know. I only know that it happens when we look outside. If we turn attention from an inner world of old, sad stories and focus on a new day, we can see what is waiting for us. It may be that we cannot grasp any good in what lies ahead. With the psalmist, we turn to the past, recalling the days God acted on our behalf: "I remember the days of long ago; I meditate on all your works and consider what your hands have done. I spread out my hands to you; my soul thirsts for you like a parched land." (Psalm 143:5-6) With arms outstretched, we catch wisdom from above that is available to those who endure hardship by hiding in God's embrace—and at the same time—stand in solidarity with other sufferers, other people who are wounded but open to God's grace.

Suffering can make us wise. Human wisdom is accumulated experience, seen from a distance, organized meaningfully into patterns that influence and affect the way we receive, perceive and relieve the world of some of its daily grind. To suffer well is to be called by God to care for his creation. Like the psalmist, we say, "Teach me to do your will, for you are my God; may your good Spirit lead me on level ground." (Psalm 143:10) What does it mean to be led by the Holy Spirit on level ground? The psalmist wanted God to preserve his life and get him out of trouble. He wanted God to silence his enemies and destroy all his foes. (Psalm 143:11-12) Where do your foes live? How can we learn to survive and to thrive while we are with other people even though they create and sustain harm that could cripple our joy?

We face suffering by turning our attention to Jesus, Author and Finisher of our faith, who, for the joy set before him, endured the cross. Scripture speaks to those who suffer: "Whatever you do, work at it with all your heart, as working for the Lord, not for human masters, since you know that you will receive an inheritance from the Lord as a reward. It is the Lord Christ you are serving. Those who do wrong will be repaid for their wrongs, and there is no favoritism." (Colossians 3:23-25) Christian maturity comes through wrestling with suffering, disappointment, injustice and practicing what Jesus said: "Father forgive them...they do not know what they are doing." (Luke 23:34) There is no shortcut to a grace-filled life. Scripture says, "Continue to work out your salvation with fear and trembling, for it is God who works in you to will and to act according to his good purpose." (Philippians 2:12b) If you do your best, whatever that is, God does his best and that is very great. We can struggle and fail; struggle and succeed. Keep trying.

Lord Jesus Christ, I can hardly imagine what it would be like to feel free from distresses that dog my heels and trip me up when I try to follow your leading. I am struggling to follow you. I ask with the psalmist that you would lead me on level ground: Holy Spirit, help. I want to see when I choose for myself ground that is full of potholes and obstacles that cripple me. Let me hear your voice. Let me breathe fresh air on a new morning. I believe each morning is new when you are in it. Open my eyes. Let me see there is a new day dawning. Even so, come Lord Jesus. I await you.

ENDNOTES

1   I am indebted to my friend Meghan McIntosh for expressing this insight. It is used with her permission.

2   See for example, *The Holy Bible* New International Version, Inclusive Language Version (London: Hodder and Stoughton, 1996); *The Jewish Study Bible*, Tanakh Translation, (London: Oxford University Press, 2004).

3   I am indebted to my friend and colleague, Cindy Westfall, for telling me this story. It is used with her permission.

4   J. William Worden, *Children and Grief* (New York: The Guilford Press, 1996), 124-135.

5   Robert Kegan, *The Evolving Self* (Cambridge: Harvard University Press, 1982), 129.

6   *Evolving Self*, 13.

7   *Evolving Self*, 131.

8   Sylvie Courtine-Denamy, *Three Women in Dark Times: Edith Stein, Hannah Arendt, Simone Weil*. G.M. Goshgarian, Trans. London: Cornell University Press, 2000, 22.

9   *Three Women*, 21.

10 It turned out to be an incorrect diagnosis, or else I was healed. I don't know which it was but I am grateful.

11 Georges Seurat, *Sunday Afternoon on the Island of La Grande Jatte*.

12 Joyce E. Bellous, *Educating Faith* (Toronto: Clements Publishing, 2006), 20-37.

13 Alister McGrath, *The Twilight of Atheism* (New York: Doubleday, 2004), 185.

14 Alan Richardson, *A Dictionary of Christian Theology* (Philadelphia: Westminster Press, 1969).

15 Sigmund Freud, *Totem and Taboo* (New York: Vintage Books, 1918), 98-129.

www.ingramcontent.com/pod-product-compliance
Lightning Source LLC
Chambersburg PA
CBHW031300090426
42742CB00007B/543

* 9 7 8 0 9 8 1 0 1 4 9 0 6 *